FINDING DELIGHT IN PEOPLE

FRONT COVER:

Jesus more delighted by a humble gesture than the sumptuous meal

One of the Pharisees asked Jesus to eat with him, and he went into the Pharisee's house and took his place at the table.

A woman in the city, who was a sinner, having learned that Jesus was eating in the Pharisee's house, brought an alabaster jar of ointment. She stood behind him at his feet, weeping, and began to bathe his feet with her tears and to dry them with her hair. Then she continued kissing his feet and anointing them with the ointment.

Now when the Pharisee who had invited him saw it, he said to himself, *If this man were a prophet, he would have known who and what kind of a woman this is who is touching him.*

Turning towards the woman Jesus said to the Pharisee: 'Simon, do you see this woman? I entered your house; you gave me no water for my feet, but she has bathed my feet with her tears and dried them with her hair. You gave me no kiss, but from the time I came in she has not stopped kissing my feet. You did not anoint my head with oil, but she has anointed my feet with ointment. Therefore I tell you, her sins, which were many, have been forgiven; hence she has shown great love.'

Luke 7:36-47

LIAM HICKEY

Finding delight in people

A ray of sunshine for every day

ST PAULS

ST PAULS Publishing
187 Battersea Bridge Road, London SW11 3AS

ISBN 085439 588 1

Set by TuKan, Fareham, Hampshire
Produced in the EC
Printed by The Guernsey Press Co. Ltd., Guernsey, C.I.

ST PAULS is an activity of the priests and brothers
of the Society of St Paul who proclaim the Gospel
through the media of social communication

Contents

To follow Christ the man is to become more human.

Second Vatican Council

God finds delight in his people.

Psalm 149

Introduction

Real people are human, not superhuman. Real people colour the world with loving attitudes. They let the light shine through them. The people I have chosen for our delight are mostly taken from the Calendar of Saints. They are lovers. I have tried to spotlight a loving attitude in their life story that might illuminate our life story.

Finding delight in people looks for a ray of sunshine for every day of the year. May the Light that enlightens every human heart warm our hearts.

Liam Hickey

January

1 JANUARY

Mary Mother of Jesus – Palestine – 1st century

Mary, pray for us now, and during the days ahead. You know the fear of pregnancy, the threat of rejection. You know the pain of misunderstanding, teenagers and family. You know the joy of wine at weddings. You know the pain of sorrow, of facing tragedy, disgrace and death. You pray for us.

2 JANUARY

Basil and Gregory – Cappadocia (Turkey) – 4th century

Both men tried the monastic life. But they were forced to get involved in the struggles of their day, defending the divinity of Christ against the Arian heretics. They both had brilliant minds, that helped to shape the Christian creed. Basil said at the end of his life that he seemed unsuccessful in everything. Perhaps at times the Church has tended to overstress the divinity and awesome holiness of Christ, but it is in fact very clear that he turns to us a face that is fully human as well as divine. Nothing genuinely human can be alien to Christ, and we should not be frightened to draw close to him (who is after all fully God) in communion. The Second Vatican Council encourages this confidence.

3 JANUARY

Genevieve – patroness of Paris – 6th century

When the city was besieged and famine raged she organised a food convoy. She persuaded the victors to spare the lives of many prisoners. She is buried in the Pantheon in Paris. St Genevieve was a practical peacemaker.

4 JANUARY

Elizabeth Seton – USA – 19th century

Elizabeth was American, a wife and a mother and a religious foundress. Two of her five children and her young husband died. She was rejected by her family because she embraced the Catholic faith during her visit to Italy. She built the first schools and orphanage for the poor in the United States. While rearing her children she also founded a religious community.

5 JANUARY

John Neumann – The Czech Republic – 19th century

John left Prague for the United States, where he was ordained a priest. In the States he devoted his life to the care of fellow immigrants. He was the first Redemptorist to take vows in the USA.

6 JANUARY

The Magi visit the manger

Looking towards the manger we see wealth – three kings from the East, and poverty – the shabby shepherds. We see saints – Mary and Joseph, and sinners – shepherds who did not attend the temple. We see the ox and the donkey. All are in harmony, and at ease with each other because of the Child. God never threatens, only loves. There is no need to be afraid.

7 JANUARY

Raymond of Penyafort – Spain – 13th century

Raymond was an expert in Church law and a tireless worker for prisoners. He was inspired by the law of love and compassion, rather than by the love of law. He lived to be a 100 years old. We worry about age, nobody grows old by number of years; rather we grow old by deserting ideals. Years wrinkle the skin, lack of enthusiasm wrinkles the soul. So long as our heart receives messages of beauty and cheer and courage and wonder from the earth, from other people, from the infinite, so long are we young.

8 JANUARY

Thorfinn – 13th century

Thorfinn was a Norwegian bishop. He had a row with the king and was banished. Years later a poem was found telling of his great qualities. He made me think of Etty Hillesum who died in the Auschwitz concentration camp in the Second World War. Her diaries were found. They tell an extraordinary story of the goodness, humanity and compassion of a girl who said that it was a voice speaking in her heart that was her motivation.

9 JANUARY

Adrian – Africa – 8th century

Adrian was an African. He turned down the See of Canterbury in favour of Theodore, but travelled with him as companion and advisor. There is great wisdom in knowing one's strength and weakness. The poet Patrick Kavanagh speaks of the wonder of weeds, and the only perfection is that of being too right and too wrong, too weak and too strong, being wild, being failure. But that is life – there is no perfection.

10 JANUARY

Agatho – Italy – 7th century

Agatho was married and a businessman. He became a monk and later Pope. He helped to restore unity between the Eastern and Western Church at the Sixth General Council at Constantinople. Do we ever really discover who we are in this life? There is so much more to us than we dream or imagine. God says we are his delight.

11 JANUARY

Theodosius – Turkey – 6th century

Theodosius built a monastery that grew into a small city with hospitals and churches. It cared for the sick, infirm and mentally disturbed. He used to dig a fresh grave every day to remind himself of death. It is unproductive, to think about death unless it helps us to appreciate life now. A man after a serious operation remarked to me. "When I woke up I saw life differently. Now I'll take more time to look at the flowers."

12 JANUARY

Benedict Biscop – England – 7th century

Benedict Biscop was born in Northumbria and travelled for God to Rome, Lerins, Canterbury. He founded monasteries at Wearmouth and at Jarrow. He introduced the first stone church building and glass windows to England, engaging French workmen. There is in all of us a Martha and a Mary, a reflective aspect and an active aspect in our personality. To keep a harmony between the two gives peace of mind.

13 JANUARY

Hilary – France – 4th century

Hilary was elected bishop of Poitiers in 350, being married with a young daughter. He fought for the truth in a Church that was split by the heresy of Arius. He was banished by the Emperor. We are not used to the idea of a bishop being married and becoming a saint, yet Hilary was one of the great men of the Christian Church. The truth is that the love of God reaches every person no matter what job one does.

14 JANUARY

Sava – Serbia – 13th century

Sava was a great peacemaker for his people. He built harmony between the monastery and the palace. While he was hard on himself, he was always gentle with others. May the spirit of Sava touch the troubled lives of the people of Serbia at this time.

15 JANUARY

Ita – Ireland – 6th century

Ita is remembered as the teacher of St Brendan the Navigator. Perhaps it was her influence that inspired Brendan to spread the Good News of God across the world. One of the great influences in my life was the local postman, who encouraged me to play football. This gave me joy and sanity, and many friends through my young life. His only request was to be remembered in prayer.

16 JANUARY

Marcellus – Italy – 4th century

There was no Pope for four years because of persecution. With the change of emperor, Marcellus, a priest, was elected by the people. He was over-anxious in reorganising a lapsed Church. He was forced into exile and death after only a few months. Often life presents situations with no easy solutions. If we are too lax we are accused of condoning wrong. If we are too severe we are accused of being pitiless and uncompassionate. St Augustine said to pray as if all depended on God and to act as if all depended on self.

17 JANUARY

Antony, the Abbot – Egypt – 4th century

Antony lived in solitude, yet he was a friend of Athanasius, who challenged the heresy of Arius. He was embarrassed to receive a letter from the Emperor Constantine seeking his advice. He said that God writes to us all the time in his Son, and those words are more important than the Emperor's letter. The Gospel story does not belong to the past. It is God speaking to us now in the circumstances of this day. The question is, where and how?

18 JANUARY

Priscilla – Rome – 1st century

With her husband she was banished from Rome because she was Jewish. She became a friend of St Paul. There is a catacomb in Rome which recalls her name. The Roman Empire was a male world, so it is extraordinary that a woman's name should be remembered to this day. Each of our names is written on the hand of God with love.

19 JANUARY

Wulfstan – England – 11th century

Wulfstan put an end to slave trade between England and Ireland. He was supported by Archbishop Landfranc of

Canterbury. Wulfstan was a Benedictine monk in Worcester. He became bishop, reluctantly, because of his concern for people. Politics and religion are both concerned with the well-being of the human person, of society and the world we live in. "I was hungry, and you gave me to eat, I was thirsty, and you gave me drink, I was in prison …" (Mt 25).

The glory of God is a person fully alive.

20 JANUARY

Fabian – Rome – 3rd century

Fabian reminds me of Simon of Cyrene and the Fifth Station of the Cross. Fabian was a layman and a farmer. He came to Rome for the day of a pope's election. A dove lit on his head, and all the clergy and people said this was a sign that Fabian should be the new pope. He remained Pope for 15 years until his martyrdom by the Emperor Decius. One day I was worried, walking along, talking to myself. A little schoolgirl ran over to me to shake my hand, and give me a hug. God has funny ways and does funny things. Such is the God of surprises!

21 JANUARY

Agnes – Rome – 3rd century

My mother's name was Agnes. I do not remember her telling us that the first Agnes was a very beautiful teenager, who was martyred because she was a Christian.

We can underestimate the goodness and generosity of young people. There is enthusiasm there that can be channelled, towards concern for people and care for our environment. It is our spirit that makes us happy, not just possession of things. Money is good in the pocket, but bad in the heart.

22 JANUARY

Vincent – Spain – 4th century

Vincent was tortured and imprisoned by the governor Decius. Whether the governor changed his mind or his heart we don't know. Vincent was released and given a comfortable bed. It was then that he collapsed and died. We sometimes think that God wants suffering or even likes suffering. Jesus did not teach this, rather he heals suffering. He endured suffering himself because it is an expression of love. To be loving persons will always involve struggle, and strain, and pain.

23 JANUARY

John the Almsgiver – Cyprus – 7th century

When his wife and children died John entered religious life. He became Patriarch of Alexandria. He was generous-hearted and peace-loving. It is said that the responsible and caring person could take on any job in life. I believe that this is true.

24 JANUARY

Francis de Sales – France – 17th century

A lawyer, priest, bishop and saint. Francis is called the "Gentleman Saint" because of his kindness. He was a brilliant teacher who used simple language and mottos like "A spoonful of honey will catch more flies than a hundred barrels of vinegar". Praise warms us. The charm of Jesus is that he saw praiseworthy things in people who were rejects and without any standing with Church or state. Francis said, "To speak well you have to love well, and if you speak too much you pick up too little."

25 JANUARY

Paul – his conversion – Palestine – 1st century

Saul, persecutor and murderer, becomes Paul, the greatest champion of God's love. Like Thomas Merton, Paul in his religious experience on the road to Damascus saw Jesus walking in love with every human person on this earth. Paul understood the human condition – our split personality, desiring one thing, often doing the opposite. His message is stunning. We are saved entirely by God, not by anything we can do. God's love is forever patient, kind, without limit. He fought with Peter, but only in defence of love being greater than ritual.

26 JANUARY

Timothy and Titus – Asia Minor (Turkey) – 1st century

Timothy and Titus were close friends of Paul on his incredible journeys. Timothy was of mixed religion and a teenager when Paul met him. Paul says, "Let no one look down on you because of your youth." He writes to him, "Stop drinking water, take a little wine for the good of your stomach." Paul's letter to Titus, his secretary, is a Christmas favourite: "When the kindness and love of God our Saviour appeared, he saved us, not because of any righteous deeds we had done, but because of his mercy" (Tit 3:4-5).

27 JANUARY

Angela Merici – Italy – 16th century

It is better to talk to God than to talk about God. Although orphaned and only thirteen years old, Angela was allowed to receive daily Communion – very exceptional in those days. She gathered together a group of women, who from their homes saw to the education of underprivileged young girls. She named her sisters – The Ursulines. Angela refused the request of Pope Clement VII to found a congregation of nursing sisters. God forces no one to obey him. God invites us to companionship. People who see God as love, and see God's love as pervasive in all that exists in life, are the best qualified to teach about God. True religion is caught rather than taught.

28 JANUARY

Thomas Aquinas – Italy – 13th century

The ambition of Thomas' mother for him was to be Benedictine Abbot of Monte Cassino. When he joined the Dominicans, she had him kidnapped and hidden for a year. During this time his sister gave him the Scriptures and books of philosophy. He became one of the greatest teachers the world has known. Thousands of students were attracted to his ideas in Paris. In his student years he was called the "dumb ox". When he was completing his master work, "The Summa", he stopped and said, "I cannot go on. All I have written seems like straw, compared to what I have seen and what has been told to me." The wonder of God cannot be caught in any single image or idea. Father, Son and Spirit are three different persons of God to whom we can pray.

29 JANUARY

Bathildis, England – 7th century

Bathildis was taken as a slave to the palace of King Clovis II in France. The king fell in love with her beauty and married her. They had three sons. When King Clovis died, she reformed the rules relating to Christian slaves. She founded monasteries. God uses the weak to confound the wise. It is often our own weakness that is a hidden blessing, that keeps us close to the earth and trusting in God's mercy.

30 JANUARY

Margaret Birmingham – Ireland – 16th century

Margaret chose harsh imprisonment in Dublin Castle, and eventual death, rather than give up her faith in the Catholic Mass. She befriended hunted priests, hiding them in her home. When her own son, who had turned priest hunter, became Mayor of Dublin, he had his mother arrested. The same Dublin Castle is resplendent today, for different reasons. It welcomes peacemaking personalities from all over the world. The silence of its stones cries out with gladness.

31 JANUARY

John Bosco – Italy – 19th century

John won the confidence of wayward young people by juggling, hand tricks, tightrope walking, playing the violin, telling stories and singing. He taught the young to write and read, and prepared them for a trade, helped by his mother, Occhiena. There was the smell of God's love in his way of life. His only discipline was loving care. Such was the influence of this kind-hearted man that the authorities allowed him to take 300 convicts from jail for a day's outing – *without a guard*. He founded the Daughters of Our Lady Help of Christians for neglected young girls. A great blessing in any community is to see interest in young people's affairs – people giving time for their activities. It is better to teach a person how to fish, than to give a person a fish. John Bosco said, "Do the best you can, God and Our Lady will do the rest."

February

1 FEBRUARY

Brigid, Ireland – 5th century

There is a taste of spring about St Brigid. She is the Celtic Goddess, turned Christian. She is Mary of the Gael. Green, riverside rushes are interwoven into her beautiful Brigid Cross. Its heart goes in four directions. For Brigid, all of life, the four corners of the earth, are interwoven with God's love in Jesus Christ. She is the saint of field and farm – the woman of hospitality. She is loved for her feminine qualities, choosing to take the veil when the "done thing" was to get married, choosing the responsibility of a bishop with the blessing of St Mel.

2 FEBRUARY

Mary Day – Candlemas

Today is the feast of candles. The candle links together all peoples, all age groups, all religions, all our intentions. Jesus Christ is our candle that Mary lights for us. Today we light a candle to carry our message, our hope, our desire to the heart of God, in the belief that Mary always prays for us, now and in our hour of need.

3 FEBRUARY

Blaise, Armenia, Turkey – 4th century

It is said that Blaise saved the life of a young boy who was choking on a fishbone. Today throats are blessed with two crossed candles and the words, "Through the intercession of St Blaise, bishop and martyr, may the Lord preserve you from all harm to your throat and every other harm. Amen." The throat – the human voice – for song and joy and speech, is an awesome gift. We are reminded of the God of surprises.

4 FEBRUARY

Dietrich Bonhoffer, Germany – 20th century

The suffering of his oppressed people called Dietrich back to Germany to speak for the dumb. The Church is only Church, he said, when it speaks for others. I am only a spoke, he said. But in a wheel of evil, I must resist. God cannot send evil, he said, rather God draws good out of evil. Even our own defects and failings are not in vain. As he became more familiar with death, every new day was a miracle. He prayed, "Help me to forgive all those from whom I have suffered." He was executed before the end of World War II.

5 FEBRUARY

Agatha – Catania, Italy – 3rd century

The St Agatha I knew worked as a nursing sister in a college boarding school, where I spent some of my teen years. My mother had died. Life was lonely; but Sister Agatha was a breath of fresh air. She always had a smile and a welcome, with a "surprise" something to eat, for a youngster who was perpetually hungry. The first Agatha was beautiful too, a white angel, martyred. Red martyrdom sheds blood, but there is the everyday white martyrdom, of people like Sister Agatha who gave so much to others in quiet, unnoticed, loving sacrifice, even for mischievous youngsters.

6 FEBRUARY

Paul Miki and Gonzalo Garcia – Japan – 16th century

Nagasaki is a city of crucifixion – the atomic bomb was dropped in 1945. Twenty-six Christians were crucified by order of the Emperor in 1597. Gonzalo Garcia was not acceptable to the Jesuits in Japan, so he left for Macao. He lived there, as a businessman and a merchant. He then joined the Franciscan brotherhood and went to Manila. He worked in the kitchen and shopped in the marketplace. When the Manila Franciscans opened a Christian mission in Japan, Gonzalo went as interpreter. Persecution broke out in Japan. Gonzalo was crucified with twenty-five others, including Paul Miki and his two Jesuit companions. It is strange the way God treats his friends. God says you are always loved unconditionally. Actions and occupation are not the measure of our worth. God's love is.

7 FEBRUARY

Theodore of Heraclea – Greece – 4th century

Theodore was a general in the Greek army. When it was discovered that he was Christian, he was beheaded. Truth is often a threat that we want to get rid of. Herod cannot face truth – John the Baptist dies. Pilate cannot face truth – Jesus dies. Standing by our commitments, being loyal, will cause pain, but it is the price of peace of mind.

8 FEBRUARY

John of Matha – France – 17th century

During Mass John had a vision of an angel holding in his arms two slaves, one white, the other dark. This inspired him to gather people together who would work to buy back Christian slaves who had been captured by the Moors. They called themselves the Trinitarians. St Louis of France supported the Trinitarians, and the Spanish poet Cervantes was a slave who was liberated by the Trinitarians. I admire Amnesty International which works for the liberation of people and freedom of conscience in today's world. Keeping holy the Sabbath Day originated with an enslaved people whose God wanted their dignity respected with a rest day. The glory of God is a human fully alive.

9 FEBRUARY

Adrian – Africa – 8th century

Adrian is buried in the historic city of Canterbury. He refused the office of Archbishop, but went to England in support of Theodore, who appointed Adrian abbot. His Christian influence from the Canterbury monastery spread far and wide, reaching out to France and Germany. It is not easy to know the job one is best suited for in life. We can never be a hundred per cent certain. There is always an element of risk and fear. If the job is something we feel happy about, and enjoy doing, generally speaking it is a good sign. But then again we have to make our own joy and happiness too. It is too much to expect others to make us happy all the time.

10 FEBRUARY

Scholastica – Italy – 6th century

Scholastica and Benedict were twins. When Benedict was abbot of Monte Cassino, Scholastica founded a Benedictine convent nearby. They met once a year, as their religious law allowed, at a halfway house. At one of their meetings Scholastica pressed Benedict to stay the night, but he was over-zealous about the rule that obliged him to return to the monastery. She had a quick word with God, and suddenly there was a violent thunderstorm; so Benedict had to stay the night. The rule of love comes before the rule of law. The Benedictine rule of love comforts the weak and challenges the strong. The twins lie buried together in Monte Cassino.

11 FEBRUARY

Our Lady of Lourdes – France – 19th century

My favourite shrine is Lourdes. It fills my mind with soothing images. The presence and sound of water. The Lady asked Bernadette to scratch the earth, and healing water flowed. It is a place of wheelchairs and stretchers where the sick are hosted, like nowhere else on earth. They take first place in all processions and celebrations. People from all over the world come together here. There is peace, hospitality, joviality in the air, and everyday market bargaining. It is a place apart. When Bernadette was hassled by the authorities about the truth of her visions, she said, "The Lady did not ask me to make anyone believe, she only asked me to tell my story." Force is never God's way – invitation is.

12 FEBRUARY

Meletius – Lesser Armenia – 4th century

Meletius is a famed peacemaker. The bitterness surrounding the heresy of Arius affects our attitude to receiving the Eucharist to this day. Meletius was chosen to be Bishop of Antioch, and tried to reunite the two parties there. He was of a gentle disposition, but strong character. His mission put him in a "no win" situation. He accepted responsibility and endured rejection. The true peacemaker gets involved in the struggle, and takes on the scars of battle. The peace lover sits on the fence, does not get involved. Parents are the first and best of peacemakers.

13 FEBRUARY

Catherine De' Ricci – Italy – 16th century

The search for peace goes on in every human heart. We long for a cure, a therapy, a touch that will help us cope with disease, addiction, illness, unhappiness and the problems of life. Catherine De' Ricci found her peace in meditating on the suffering and passion of Jesus Christ. She experienced ecstasy for some hours every Thursday and Friday for twelve years. She prayed that the ecstasies would stop, because of the crowds that came to see her, including three future popes. Although her prayers were healing for others, she herself died after a long illness. Many people find peace of mind in sitting quietly for a few minutes a day, doing nothing, saying nothing – just being. Jesus went to the hills alone to pray.

14 FEBRUARY

Valentine – Italy – 3rd century

Love is in the air. The swallows are back at this time. Father Sprat was a Dubliner of extraordinary love and spring-like liveliness. He became a Carmelite in Cordoba, Spain. Returning to Dublin he became a saint of the slums. He was also a brilliant orator. Invited to Rome to preach in the Jesuit Church, he was so impressive, that Pope Gregory XVI presented him with the remains of St Valentine for Ireland. The martyr's body was transferred from St Hippolytus Cemetery in Rome to the Carmelite Church in Whitefriar Street in Dublin on 10 November

1836. The candles that lovers light today at St Valentine's Shrine are reminders that we are sparks of God's love, and that we can light the world with goodness and friendships.

15 FEBRUARY

Jordan of Saxony and Diana d'Andalo – Italy – 13th century

Some years ago I wrote a note to Cardinal Thomas O'Fiaich, Primate of Ireland in Armagh. I complimented him on his televised Christmas message. He wrote back saying, "You have no idea how much joy your wee note gave me. I rarely get letters of compliment, and never from the clergy. I got one other letter complaining at the luxurious chair I was sitting on during the TV interview." Jordan of Saxony and Diana d'Andalo carried on a friendship through letter writing for more than fifteen years. The unexpected card or note received in friendship is a taste of God.

16 FEBRUARY

Onesimus – Palestine – 1st century

Onesimus was a slave of Philemon. Philemon was a convert of St Paul. Onesimus ran away. He met Paul in a Roman prison. He became a Christian under his influence. Paul returned him to Philemon with a goodwill letter – all was forgiven. A change of heart, a change in the right direction can bring great blessings. Jesus was always inviting people to turn around, to look at life another way – a man had two sons, a man fell among robbers, a woman is humiliated. And the psychologist said we ask ourselves the wrong questions. To return hurt for hurt – is that the only option?

17 FEBRUARY

Servite Founders – Italy – 13th century

Seven young men in fashionable Florence decided to leave job and home. They called themselves Servants of Mary – loving God through prayer and serving the needs of people. A friend of mine has chosen to be a hermit on the slopes of Croagh Patrick in Co. Mayo. Young people often ask me about her – isn't her solitude a waste of time and life? The hermit would say, yes, I suppose I have chosen the easier way. The challenge of business life, of marriage and children is more difficult and blessed, but God asked me to do this, to be a sign and reminder that we are worth more than what we do or what we have, or how fashionable we are. God is love and God is the reason of all our fruitfulness.

18 FEBRUARY

Fra Angelico – Italy – 15th century

Priest and great artist, Fra Angelico enriched our world with his masterpieces. It is said that everybody can paint, because every person has an inner passion and creativity. We take photographs with our imagination all the time. Painting is an expression on canvas of an idea, an emotion. It is a spirit thing, embellished with coloured earth by a loving artist. A painting is a mini incarnation. Jesus Christ becomes fleshed with our human earthiness, because of the kindness of the Supreme Loving Artist, and he dwells among us. I am with you always. A painting is a spirit dwelling among us.

19 FEBRUARY

Conrad – Italy – 14th century

On a hunting expedition Conrad lit a fire that went out of control and destroyed a lot of property. A woodcutter was wrongly accused, and condemned to death. Conrad, to make amends for his action, sold off all his possessions and with his wife entered religious life. There are three "R" instructions on the golf course: repair, replace, rake. We can repair hurt with words like, "I'm sorry, I did not mean it". We can replace loss by giving time and help to others in the community, making a better world. We can rake out bitterness and prejudice with the helping hand of God's Spirit.

20 FEBRUARY

Eucherius – France – 8th century

Eucherius desired the monastic life. But the people of Orleans wanted him as their bishop. He wanted his monks to hide him, but the people prevailed. He was exiled to Cologne by Charles Martel for defending church property and later sent to Liege. He retired to a monastery to die. What to do in life, where to go, is not often easy to know. Sometimes circumstances chart our course, sometimes we chose our ways. The only certainty is that God's love pervades all our comings and goings. Every turn and twist on the road of life is in his providence.

21 FEBRUARY

Peter Damien – Italy – 11th century

As a young lad Peter had to mind pigs. He was orphaned and poor. Although he loved solitude he became very active with his reforms within Church and state. He had a brilliant mind, which he expressed in his writing and lecturing. I like his sense of humour. For his own obituary he wrote: "What you are I was. What I am you will be. Remember me. I pray for you. Have mercy on Peter."

22 FEBRUARY

Margaret of Cortona – Italy – 13th century

Margaret ran off with her lover. He was killed tragically nine years later. She was left with her faithful dog and a little child. She decided to give her whole life to the poor and sick. She had great attraction for all kinds of sinners. The Easter Poet calls our Adam and Eve story a "happy fall". Because of our very failures, inconsistencies and crushed spirit, the heart of God is touched. We are embraced rather than condemned. Weeds of temptation touched by the sunshine of love can be transformed. There is no virtue without temptation.

23 FEBRUARY

Polycarp – Smyrna, Turkey – 2nd century

Polycarp was appointed bishop by John the Apostle. He agreed to disagree with the Pope about the date of Easter. To keep one's conviction while respecting the conviction of others is a way to peace. Before martyrdom, when asked to deny Christ, he said: "I have served him 86 years. Never did he fail me. Why should I deny him now?"

24 FEBRUARY

Walburga – England – 8th century

Boniface, the great apostle of Germany, was the uncle of Walburga. He invited her and her religious community from Wimborne in England, to help with evangelisation in Germany. She was an outstanding missionary and a prodigious writer during her years in Bavaria. In today's world of technology England and Germany are only seconds or minutes apart. It prompts the thought that we are all rooted to something or someone greater than the individual places we live in. Exaggerated nationalism does not make for harmony of humanity.

25 FEBRUARY

Tarasius – Constantinople – 9th century

Tarasius was a layman and secretary to the Empress Irene. He was chosen as Patriarch of Constantinople by popular demand. He restored holy images as a way of devotion during the controversy over icons. He also confronted the Emperor when he tried deceitfully to divorce his wife, the Empress Mary. Conscience is sacred for every person and is the voice of God. But it is a voice that is heard through the wisdom of listening to his Spirit in the Church. It is not simply doing one's own thing.

26 FEBRUARY

Alexander – Alexandria – 4th century

People are welcomed to the table of the Lord, not because of virtue but because of human weakness and the goodness of God in Jesus Christ. Jesus welcomed sinners, strays and rejects. He sits and eats with us. Alexander defended the divinity of Jesus. Arius, a priest, denied that Jesus could be divine. The ripples of this controversy effect our lives to this day. People stay away from celebrating the sacraments of God saying: "We are not good enough." True, we are never good enough, but the Christian faith is about God's goodness and God's love for us – warts and all. God always invites – come take and eat.

27 FEBRUARY

Gabriel Possenti – Italy – 19th century

A priest was giving advice about reading the Gospel and the Scriptures in public. He said hear the Gospel, understand what is being said and make us be moved. We have to work at the hearing and the understanding, but being moved is letting God's love touch us and make us loving. This is deeply mysterious. Gabriel Possenti was a lover of life, but a reluctant lover of God. One day during a Lady of Sorrows Festive Procession in his native Spoleto the eyes of the Madonna met his. He was a captive from then on. It was love at first sight. That love took over his life.

28 FEBRUARY

Romanus – Italy – 5th century

Romanus wanted to get away from it all. He went to the mountains to be alone. His brother found him, and later his sister and friends joined up. There is a price to pay for the quiet life. Jesus tried to get away too, but when they found him, he had compassion for the crowd. Parents with little children can never get away from it all. Their work and time are surely blessed. We can look at inevitable happenings of life as obstacles or opportunities. Better to believe that opportunity knocks.

29 FEBRUARY

The Leap Year Saints

It seems a bit unfair to be born on the 29th of February… missing out on the yearly celebration. Yet, I suspect that the leap year people celebrate with greater enthusiasm every fourth year. We forgetful humans can take so much for granted in life with the ordinary everyday… every year blessings… the sunlight that travels 94 million miles everyday to greet us, the wonders of nature that sing to us… "I am here for you", the people that surround us with blessings almost unnoticed, parents, family, relations, neighbours, clubs, teams, services of all kinds, shop, travel, hospital and country. Absence, they say, makes the heart grow fonder. Absence also can make more joyful celebration, so thanks to the leap year saints who keep reminding us of our blessings.

March

1 MARCH

David – Wales – 6th century

David is patron of Wales. It is said that he confronted the thorny question which Pelagius had raised of how free we are. St Paul said that he longed to do the good, but found himself doing the opposite through human weakness. We are flawed, but loved unconditionally by God. We are graced sinners, with a great capacity to redeem one another. Minds and emotions are often deeply wounded by wrong attitudes about God passed down to us. These can paralyse our relationship with the all-loving Father. We need to read the Gospel stories with new eyes.

2 MARCH

Chad – England – 7th century

Chad was accused of being improperly ordained Bishop of York. When the Archbishop of Canterbury challenged him, he said that he had never been fit for the job anyway. His only interest was God and loving God's people. Good Pope John XXIII had words of wisdom: unity in essentials, openness to non-essentials, charity overall. He said that we could get too fussy over non-essentials. The essential is God's love for us, our care for one another.

3 MARCH

Katherine Drexel – USA – 20th century

Katherine was a wealthy American woman. She met Pope Leo XIII in Rome during a visit to Europe. She asked him to send missionaries to the poor and underprivileged in America. The Pope said: "Why don't you become a missionary yourself?" She did. She gave her twelve million dollars to build schools and missions to educate the less fortunate throughout the USA.

Kathy and Valerie are young mothers who help in our local church. They felt shy and unqualified without catechetical certificates. But they did have a real love for the children and a desire to help them to grow lovingly as human beings. There were smiles, handshakes and praise. The words and explanations fitted easily into the warmth of that love.

4 MARCH

Casimir – Poland – 15th century

Casimir is patron of Poland. He was the son of the King. But he refused to go to battle because he believed the words of Jesus: "Blessed are the peacemakers." They told me how they missed granddad around the home at Christmas time. He was a great peacemaker, almost unnoticed. He told the little ones stories. He settled rows with the older ones. He listened to the adults giving out about neighbours and relations and he cooled their tempers. He went to the shop for groceries and brought the dog for a walk. True peacemaking always involves putting oneself out.

5 MARCH

John Joseph of the Cross – Italy – 17th century

John was very hard on himself with his prayer and fasting, but he was easy on his followers, advising them to make sure of their recreation every day. Being compassionate and merciful is a real taste of God. When the prodigal returned his older brother could not participate in the celebrations and dancing because he was so resentful, but the father had equal compassion on him too.

6 MARCH

Colette – France – 15th century

It is the way of life that we get tired, get stale and can lose touch. We can resent change of any kind. Yet there is no growth without change. Not to change is to die. Colette breathed new life into her decaying family of religious Sisters called the Poor Clares. She was deeply resented by many, but her love of God and the goodness of people kept her on course.

"How can I get my teen children to go to Mass?" the mother asked the lecturer. Not by argument, not by attack, he said. You sit down and listen, without interruption and tolerantly, to their reasons for not going. (You'll find yourself agreeing with many of their reasons, even though some are not very well thought out.) Then they will sit down and listen, without interruption and tolerantly, to your reasons for going to Mass. When there is challenge and tolerance there is room for the Spirit to move, but even if nothing happens you still keep the door open.

7 MARCH

Perpetua and Felicity – Italy – 3rd century

Both chose love of their new-found Saviour, Jesus Christ, even though the price was loss of family and even their own children, and finally death in the arena. God's love has often been called a consuming fire, that is greater than reason. We avoid pain, suffering and death as evil. Jesus came to heal and save and to break the power of evil and death. He did not choose pain, but it was the price of loving. Listening to children, loyalty to a partner, praise for another, are the ingredients of love.

8 MARCH

John of God – Portugal – 16th century

John of God was a man of many parts, a shepherd, a soldier, a seller of religious books. He beat himself up once in a rage and did time in a lunatic asylum. There he was advised to devote his energies to needy people, so in his forties he began to set up night shelters for the poor, the sick and homeless. He used to say, "For God's sake do yourself a good turn." John was accused of consorting with tramps and prostitutes. He explained to the Archbishop that Jesus Christ was a friend of prostitutes and tax collectors. They would not have accepted Jesus unless he spoke their language. I am unfaithful to my vocation if I don't speak the language of the poor and underprivileged, he said.

9 MARCH

Frances of Rome – Italy – 15th century

There is a Martha and Mary in all of us, we are active yet reflective. All work and no reflection is unbalanced and all reflection with no work is no earthly use. Frances got the balance right. There are times, she said, when you have to leave aside your devotions at the altar to be devoted to the duty of the home. The service of pots and pans, babies and teenagers, rows and discussions. The everyday routine is God's work, the stuff of life. She did not want to marry, but made a good success of marriage. She kept a good home, yet found time, with others, for the sick, the poor and the unfortunate. God walked with her and she walked with God.

10 MARCH

John Ogilvie – Scotland – 16th century

In the movie *Shine* a well-meaning parent tries to over control his son's musical genius. The son breaks from the home, shines into stardom and then collapses with mental disturbance. He loses one kind of shine, but gains another kind which is full of humour and joy. When the parents of John Ogilvie sent their son to further studies in Europe they never dreamed that he would break from his Calvinist tradition to become a Catholic. He was then seventeen years of age and later was ordained a Jesuit priest. He came back to his native Scotland in disguise to minister to persecuted people. He was betrayed and hanged in Glasgow this day 1615.

11 MARCH

Eulogius – Spain – 9th century

The cities of Cordova and Toledo are amongst the best delights of Spain. The warm air is heavy with history. The very stones speak of Saracen invasions, Moorish culture and art alongside Christian endurance and faith. Eulogius was a man of both cities. He was imprisoned for his Christian faith in Cordova, and later appointed Archbishop of Toledo. He never took up that duty. He was beheaded for trying to help a Moorish girl, Leocritia, who had become a Christian. Moors and Christians were lovers of water and light, expressions of beauty. Why should differences divide us when there is so much we have in common – essential beauty, water, air, light and blood.

12 MARCH

Theophanes – Constantinople – 9th century

We live in a world of images and icons. It is not easy to understand why people fought wars over sacred images. Perhaps Emperor Leo V in 814 felt that his image was the all-important one and that other images were a threat to his security. Theophanes ignored the Emperor's ruling against icons, so he was condemned, scourged and imprisoned. He died in exile. He was a married man who became a monk. He is a saint of East and West. I marvel at the images of photography that befriend our world. The good memories of old photos, the everyday snap celebrates the joys of life, the happenings of our times.

13 MARCH

Euphrasia – Constantinople – 5th century

It is not uncommon to blame others – family, teacher, church, for our own inadequacies. Some suggest that it is our genes only that condition our behaviour. I don't think that Euphrasia would agree. She was set up to marry into nobility, but she chose to be a nun. She wrote to the Emperor Arcadius requesting that her family wealth be used for the poor and the release of prisoners and that she be allowed to follow her decision. He agreed. It is our own decisions that make life. Life is in our own hands under the providence of God.

14 MARCH

Matilda – Germany – 10th century

Most of her young life was lived in a monastery with her grandmother. She was given to Henry in marriage. He became king of Germany. Her son Otto became Emperor. Her generosity and charity was so liberal that her sons Otto and Henry had her banished from the royal court. Power and authority are meant for responsibility and service. Matilda's love for the poor and underprivileged gave balance to her authority, but not perfection to her judgements.

15 MARCH

Louise de Marillac – France – 17th century

She was married and busy, widowed and worried about her son Michael. She became the angel with a human face for the poor on the streets of Paris. Under the inspiration of St Vincent de Paul she left the world the legacy of the Daughters of Charity. Their dress was that of the peasant women of France. Their work was wherever there was human need and suffering, among children, the aged, the infirm and the insane. Her prayer was love the poor, honour them as you would Christ himself.

16 MARCH

John de Brébeuf – France – 17th century

The French and English and native Indians set the political scene in Canada in the days of John de Brébeuf. He wanted to be a missionary among the Indians. When a fatal disease struck the Indians their tribes blamed the missionaries for the disaster. John was murdered. He had composed a dictionary and catechism for the Huron Indians before his death. There are no ideal situations in politics, religion or life. But it is better to light a candle than to curse the darkness. It is easy to sit on the fence and criticise all and everything. It takes real integrity to get involved, to do something, to lift a hand, to say a word. Cynicism is corrosive.

17 MARCH

Patrick – Britain – 5th century

Patrick is patron of Ireland. When he was kidnapped he became a shepherd. He escaped to France and later returned to Ireland in response to the voices of people calling him back to tell the Good News of Jesus Christ. Patrick believed in God's pervasive presence in all that exists, in mountain and stream, in people and sacred books, in chapels and cells. He baptised the best traditions of the Celtic way of life. Rather than rejecting difference, he simply placed the resurrected Christ in the centre of life – in him we live, move and have our being. The triple spiral of Newgrange of 5,000 BC became the

Triple Trinity of the Shamrock for Patrick. God is the source of all – full of life and light, fertility and water. The God in three persons – Father, Son and Spirit – to whom we pray with never-ending variety. The Christian God is full of surprises.

18 MARCH

Cyril of Jerusalem – Jerusalem – 4th century

In the early days after Vatican II, there was enthusiasm and freshness in the air. Sister Romaine used to remind us that if we catch this Good News of Jesus Christ and the spirit of the Council, life will never be the same. You will probably suffer much, she said, from others who don't want to change and see no value in renewal. Some will feel safer with the God of threats, with the overstress on evil and sin in the world, rather than the God of surprises and joy who invites us to build his Kingdom now and make a better world even with our limitations and even through our limitations. Cyril of Jerusalem had the mind of a Sister Romaine. He was a good news man, who suffered much because he sold church property to help the poor in time of famine. He also took a strong stand on the God of Love who suffers and who identifies with weak humanity, rather than the authoritarian God who rules from far away.

19 MARCH

Joseph – Palestine – 1st century

Joseph was husband of Mary the mother of Christ. He was loyal to Mary despite the unusual circumstances of her pregnancy. He took responsibility. He endured the pain of exile for Mary and their child. He provided for the family at Nazareth. Every family is a holy family because family is God's idea. Loyalty, responsibility, the ordinary routine of everyday caring are the ingredients of family living. They are gifts, wrapped and tied, with love inside.

20 MARCH

Cuthbert – England – 7th century

Melrose, Ripon, Lindisfarne speak of Cuthbert and his integrity. His loyalty to the Celtic tradition on the date of Easter reminds me of the dedication of people to the Latin Mass and the old ritual that reverenced the sacred. When the Roman rule fixing the date of Easter was approved at the Synod of Whitby, Cuthbert was equally loyal in changing his allegiance and attitude in favour of the Roman rule. The spirit of Vatican II renewed the Mass and sacraments of the Church, with vernacular language and fuller participation of the people in the celebration. But change is never easy and often painful, yet without change there is no growth, no renewal of the seasons of life. The dried skins cannot contain the new wine.

21 MARCH.

Nicholas de Flue – Switzerland – 15th century

Nicholas was a brilliant soldier, farmer and citizen, and the father of ten children. He decided to become a hermit with the consent of his wife. He put his family affairs in order and retired to the solitude of a cell in the mountains. He broke his solitude only once to help his country when there was a danger of civil war. His prayer was: "O God, take from me all that keeps me from you. O God, give me all that brings me nearer to you. O God take myself from me and let me possess only you." He was a man of all seasons.

22 MARCH

Nicholas Owen – England – 17th century

The movie ***Schindler's List*** tells the story of how one man saved the lives of many Jewish people by his "hiding ingenuity" during World War II. Nicholas Owen ran a Schindler's Ark, hiding Catholic priests during the reign of James I. He eventually sacrificed his own life rather than betray a priest. Our lives are not tested in such dramatic ways. But our loyalties are challenged by everyday happenings. There is the temptation to run with what's popular, simply take the soft option, give in to jealousy or prejudice, rather than stand for truth and honesty.

23 MARCH

Toribio of Lima – Spain – 16th century

Majorca, Salamanca, Granada, celebrate Turibius. A layman, he was appointed Archbishop of Lima, Peru. Although son of a powerful nation and delegate of a strict Church he defended the rights of the Indian people. He learned their language out of respect for their traditions. He did all his visiting on foot. He emptied himself, taking the form of a servant.

24 MARCH

Irenaeus – Smyrna – 2nd century

Being heavenly minded but no earthly use is not a compliment. There is no pie in the sky that is not cooked on earth, is nearer to the truth. The earth is good, the body a blessing. But neither are good enough alone to satisfy the longings of the human spirit. Irenaeus took on the opposition who argued that material things and the body were evil. Irenaeus thought that the glory of God is a human fully alive. The word of God never ceases coming to humanity. Yet, Irenaeus was not naive. He said the human race began as a foolish child, easily allowing itself to be deceived. It had to undergo the experience of death so as to become aware of its own finiteness, so as to be open to the God of eternal life.

25 MARCH

Margaret Clitherow – England – 16th century

I first heard of Margaret Clitherow during student holidays in the beautiful city of York. She is remembered lovingly in its stones and in its streets. She was a beautiful and witty wife and mother. She became Catholic after marriage to her well-to-do Protestant husband. She sheltered fugitive priests and for this reason forfeited her life. Her husband John pleaded for her: "Let them take all I have, but save her, for she is the best wife in all England and the best Catholic." The ideal marriage relationship is described as two hands touching together gently and firmly, not intertwined in each other, but each with its unique identity, both pointing in one direction – the unseen God of Love.

26 MARCH

Braulio – Spain – 7th century

Holy Week celebrations in Seville recall Braulio. He was a young pupil of St Isidore. They were good friends. A friend is someone who bucks you up when life is low. A friend is not blind to one's faults, but praises one's good points. Friendship is not confined or restricted by old age. It is an ambition in growing old, to grow more friendly.

27 MARCH

Rupert – Salzburg, Austria – 8th century

Rupert is a name remembered in Ireland and Austria. Perhaps it was his mother's influence which made him rename the old town of Juvavum to be the new city of Salzburg. He loved its people with the earthly concerns of humanity. He helped develop the salt mines of Salzburg for the well-being of the people.

28 MARCH

Gontran – Burgundy – 6th century

Although Gontran divorced one wife, and had the doctor advising another wife executed at her request, his people honoured him for his care and charity. Sometimes people who reform themselves, perhaps by giving up drink or smoking, can become hard and intolerant. Not so Gontran. He was very caring for his people when he reformed. It is a true test.

29 MARCH

Joseph of Arimathea – Palestine – 1st century

In Tintoretto's masterpiece, *Christ Being Taken Down from the Cross*, Joseph of Arimathea is painted with his back to us, but in brilliant colour. He is a strong and helpful presence, but we don't see his face. So much goodness is never acknowledged or seen in this life. It does not have a face – caring parents, conscientious teachers, generous people in the community, organisers of games for young people. Results are hidden from us. Often, perhaps, gratefully. Doing the job in hand for its own sake, its own worth, is indeed a blessing to be longed for.

30 MARCH

John Climacus – Syria – 6th century

John was a hermit. He was selected Abbot of Mount Sinai at 75 years of age. He resigned after four years to return to his monastery. It is said that he never contradicted anyone or had a dispute with anyone. The great Teresa of Avila, at the end of her busy life, said that she now only gave compliments. She did not see faults, and she wondered if that was laziness or goodness.

31 MARCH

Guy of Pomposa – Italy – 11th century

The habit maketh not the man. Clothes are necessary and good. But it is the person who wears the style who is more important. The human body is an awesome gift. The great Michelangelo tried to capture the spirit that enhances and inspires the human form. If there is no body, there is no spirit. Guy of Pomposa liked fancy dress, but decided to become a monk. He gave away all his clothes and lived like a beggar.

April

1 APRIL

Hugh of Grenoble – France – 11th century

We are not always the best judge of our own gifts and abilities, nor indeed of our own misgivings. Hugh was encouraged, if not pushed, into high ecclesiastical responsibility because of his gifted character. A layman, made bishop, he served four years and retired to a monastery because he felt a failure. The Pope ordered him back to his diocese and the four succeeding popes turned down his requests to be relieved of his responsibilities. He gave land to set up a Carthusian monastery under St Bruno.

2 APRIL

Francis of Paola – Italy – 15th century

A child of destiny. He was ordered by the Pope to leave his country and monastery to go to the sickbed of King Louis XI in Paris. Although renowned for his miracles, even raising the dead, he did not cure the fearful king. But he healed his mind and heart. The king died peacefully in his arms. A right attitude to death is perhaps a better miracle than a cure. Thinking about death can be a blessing if it encourages us to live well the day at our disposal, with a kind word, a helping hand and a forgiving heart.

3 APRIL

Richard of Chichester – England – 13th century

God is faithful, Richard said, and if we serve him faithfully he will provide for all our needs. Richard was faithful in his longing for true wisdom. He studied in Paris, Oxford and Bologna. He was faithful to his friend St Edmund of Canterbury and went with him into exile in France. He was faithful to his Church and people. As Bishop of Chichester he clashed with King Henry III over the appointment of bishops to vacant sees.

4 APRIL

Isidore – Seville, Spain – 6th century

Isidore is a patron of Seville. He brought many Arians back to the Catholic faith. Although he was a brilliant scholar and educator, as a child he did not like school. One day he skipped school. As he sat in the woods, he noticed how the constant drip of water wore a hole through hardened rock. Gentle perseverance can break the hardest resistance. This wisdom influenced his life to the advantage of others.

5 APRIL

Vincent Ferrer – France – 14th century

We sometimes pretend shock when religious people in high places do odd things. How about two men fighting with each other for the honour of the Papacy and dividing people's loyalty in their struggle? That was the world of Vincent Ferrer. Vincent was a friend of Benedict XIII, whom he supported as antipope in Avignon. Meantime Urban was the legitimate Pope in Rome. Later Vincent saw his mistake and pleaded with his friend, Benedict XIII, to resign. Vincent was world-famous for his effective preaching – he predicted the end of the world. Even saints are limited and human in their vision, but they are always preachers of God's love and mercy.

6 APRIL

William of Aebelholt – France – 12th century

A little bird flew into the room. It kept dashing desperately against a closed window in search of freedom. It kept missing the neighbouring window that was wide open. Jesus was always wanting to free people from tunnel vision. He used the word "repent". It means turn around. Look at life differently. Change your attitude and thinking. William was a man who could change for love's sake. He left France at the invitation of the bishop to reform Danish monasteries. His insight was right, although the road was a rocky road.

7 APRIL

John Baptist de la Salle – France – 17th century

There is much discussion nowadays on how to cope with youth and vandalism, joy-riding, drug-taking. Some opt for punishment and blame. John opted for education of the young poor. He got together a group of Brothers to provide education for the deprived. He met with great opposition from the Jansenists. He linked his education and respect for life with the Mass. While religious education today cannot be imposed on people, good religion that sees God as Loving Father and encourages people to love each other is a great boon for human development and the making of a better world.

8 APRIL

Julie Billiart – France – 18th century

Julie was paralysed for twenty-two years due to shock. One day a priest asked her to take one step in the name of the Sacred Heart of Jesus. She was instantly cured. She got together the Sisters of Notre Dame de Namur to care for young people. She housed fugitive priests during the days of the Revolution. God always hears our prayer. But he does not always do what we want. Sometimes a good attitude to life, to people, to sickness, is a better miracle than an instant cure.

9 APRIL

Mary the wife of Clopas – Jerusalem – 1st century

Mary was present at the crucifixion of Jesus. She may have been the Mary who accompanied Mary Magdalen on Easter morning to the tomb of Christ. A friend in need is a friend indeed. Mary the wife of Clopas understood the real meaning of friendship. Standing by during the sad moments. Happy for Mary Magdalen, who saw the Lord on Easter Day. The Christian person, St Paul says, rejoices with those who rejoice and is sad with those who are sorrowful.

10 APRIL

Fulbert – Italy – 10th century

Fulbert accepted responsibility as Bishop of Chartres, very reluctantly. People came from all over Europe to him for enlightenment. Ignorance is darkness. Good education enlightens the mind and activates the heart. Jesus said, "go and teach." The message is: God is Love, love one another.

11 APRIL

Stanislaus – Poland – 11th century

Stanislaus, Bishop of Krakow, is patron of Poland. He confronted King Boleslaus for his cruelties and corruption. Boleslaus killed him while he was celebrating Mass. The genuine peacemaker gets involved in the struggle for human rights and justice, but does not use violence. Violence kills, intransigence destroys unity, but love conquers.

12 APRIL

Julius 1st – Italy – 4th century

The human spirit longs for intimacy. Jesus Christ is the God of intimacy. Not a far-away outsider, who only judges and condemns. Without a God of intimacy, prayer and friendship are difficult. Jesus said: "You are my friends." It was Athanasius who defended for us the truth that the God of Intimacy became human. Arius and the emperors denied that such human intimacy could co-exist with a divine presence. Pope Julius I confirmed the stand and teaching of Athanasius through all his trials and exiles. The human and divine link arms easily in the mind of the poet Joseph Mary Plunkett: "I see his blood upon the rose and in the stars the beauty of his eyes. I see his face in every flower – the singing of the birds are his voice, rocks are his written words."

13 APRIL

Margaret of Castello – Italy – 4th century

Every family is God's family. But no family is perfect. Margaret experienced rejection from her parents because she was born defective, without sight and hunchbacked. They seemed unable to cope, but the neighbours rallied to her help. They gave her affection and love. There are so many unsung saints who give so much love to life, like foster parents, adoptive parents, grandparents, people minding children, people who have sacrificed life and time to be with another.

14 APRIL

Benedict Labre – France – 18th century

Benedict tramped the road all his adult life. One of fifteen children, he had to get used to fending for himself. He was known as the beggar of Rome and was familiar with rubbish. He dossed in the Colosseum at night. He frequented the churches of Rome during the day to pray. God's tastes are mysteriously different and beautiful. Benedict said: "I have only to desire God and heaven to get there." Such is God's mercy.

15 APRIL

Damien the Leper – Belgium – 19th century

Jesus Christ touched the untouchables. It is through touch that we express love, affection, emotion. Damien volunteered not only to work with, but, to live among, the untouchables, the incurable lepers. He went to the island of Molokai. One day he realised that he was now a leper among lepers. He was happy. The scourge of Aids scares us today. We can become afraid of touch. Not so children: they like to shake hands. They love the assurance of a hug. May the children lead us with their example?

16 APRIL

Bernadette – France – 19th century

The flowers are blooming now. They were humble seeds months ago. But they allowed themselves to be used by earth, sun and sky. The result is fragrance for the world. Bernadette, Our Lady's friend, called herself God's sweeping brush, to be used to give God's love to others. We all hurt sometimes at the thought of being used. But most of us are gifted with reasonable health and some talents. It is a privilege to have the opportunity to better the world by sharing a talent, helping another. Bernadette found peace and joy.

17 APRIL

Stephen Harding – England – 12th century

Very often we don't see the effects of our work during our lifetime. Often we see what seems collapse or failure. This is true in family life and also in single life. Stephen Harding put immense effort into founding a monastery. It was on the verge of collapse when a young horse rider with thirty men arrived at the monastery gate asking to be admitted to religious life. The young horse rider was a man called Bernard, who became one of the greatest of the Cistercian monks.

18 APRIL

Galdinus – Italy – 12th century

Galdinus loved his city of Milan. Milan laid claim to the relics of the Magi who came from the east to visit the Christ Child. The Church in Milan clashed with Frederick the Emperor. He had the relics and Galdinus removed into exile. While change is a law of life, old customs and traditions deserve respect. A man once advised: "Never say how terrible about anybody or anything, rather say how interesting."

19 APRIL

Leo 9th – France – 11th century

Leo was an army commander. He became bishop and Pope by popular appeal. As Pope he led an army against the Normans. He was defeated and captured. He introduced the idea that cardinals alone should elect a Pope. The story is told of a parish priest who requested that there be no eulogy at his funeral. He said that he did not want one person lying in the pulpit while the other person was lying in the coffin. We all have gifts and blessings from God, but we also have hidden skeletons in our human cupboards that only God knows about. We rely on God's mercy and compassion. This is the only certainty.

20 APRIL

Cyriacus – Italy – 4th century

The trees are happy that God chose their family for the Saviour's cross. What kind of wood was it? Where did it grow? What happened to it afterwards? Cyriacus, it is said, knew the hiding place of the true cross and told the Empress Helena in a dream. Through the cross is resurrection and life, that is a Christian belief. At Pilgrim Day in Clonmacnoise we were encouraged to touch the Cross of the Scriptures and try to span its huge body with our arms. St Colmcille's cross at Durrow fills the space with peace. There is a restful emptiness, full of immortal longing. Millions of voices, encouraging voices, speak in silence.

21 APRIL

Anselm – Italy – 11th century

Anselm was a runaway from home, a wanderer, a scholar, a monk, a politician. His name is linked with Normandy, Canterbury, Westminster. A defender of human rights, he negotiated a law at Westminster forbidding the sale of slaves. We think slave traffic barbaric today. Yet there are all kinds of slavery that oppress human beings now. We can be possessed, not only by what others do to us, but by our own weakness. For Anselm, true freedom is found in Jesus Christ, who invites us into "a loving" that is patient and kind, tolerant, peacemaking, generous, compassionate and joyous.

22 APRIL

Caius – Dalmatia – 3rd century

He became Pope in 283 AD. He decreed that a man must be ordained priest first, before being raised to bishop. He died in a cave in exile. We are used to the idea of a man being a priest first, before being bishop. But it was not always so. Indeed many cardinals in the Church have been lay people. In the changing world of today many people think that the priest idea is changing too, that this caring ministry of Christ can be exercised by responsible and caring lay people – single and married, male and female.

23 APRIL

George – Palestine – 4th century

George has universal appeal in East and West. He is claimed patron of many countries and cities – Palestine, Germany, England, Portugal, Greece, Aragon, Genoa, Venice. He is the one who fights evil, kills the dragon and saves the people. We humans are capable of such lofty thoughts and actions, yet we do some desperate deeds to ourselves and to others. There is a strange mix of dragon and angel in the human heart. There is bad in the best of us and good in the worst of us. Even St Paul said that while he desired to do good and hated evil, yet he did evil things. We need one to save us. Mercifully we are given Jesus Christ our Saviour. He knows that the spirit is willing and the flesh is weak. We rely on God's blessing and mercy always. We are assured of his grace and compassion.

24 APRIL

Fidelis of Sigmaringen – Germany – 16th century

Fidelis was a lawyer. He changed his job and also his name. He became a priest. He had an enthusiasm for preaching. He wanted to communicate the word of God, during the very difficult days of the post-Reformation Church. He gave his life for his dream. The word of God can be thought of as a love letter, that touches not just the mind, but warms the heart. Then there is an enthusiasm to tell others – to share the joyful news that God is compassion and love. Maybe we think too much of religion in terms of learning things and giving answers. The heart is a lonely hunter. There is a hunger of spirit. Many would say that our world is more spiritual, but less religious today. The word of God is food for the spirit.

25 APRIL

Mark – Jerusalem – 1st century

Mark is a great name. He wrote down Peter's story about Jesus. He disagreed with Paul, but was reconciled. He gives dramatic descriptions of Jesus healing the blind as if Peter is the eyewitness reporting. Peter's inability to accept a suffering Christ looms large in Mark's story. Peter's own failure and denial are not underplayed, but all is healed through the resurrection. There is no escape from suffering and darkness in life. But all is transfigured through the suffering, death and resurrection of Jesus Christ. The prayer of Mark is, "Lord, by your cross and resurrection, you have set us free. You are the Saviour of the world."

26 APRIL

Alda – Italy – 14th century

Alda was a young widow. I am sure that the death of her loved one made her feel helpless and shattered. The pain of loss and separation brings us to our knees. We wonder what to do, how to go on. Alda would say that after all the helps and therapies we have to love and adore in a new way. This means doing things now that for years we put off doing or were unable to do. My widowed friend learned to drive a car when her husband died. This gives her a new freedom. Also there can be time to do things for others, to tell others in family and community that we love them. We can make time to pray. The word "adore" means bending and there is always bending in genuine love.

27 APRIL

Zita – Italy – 13th century

Housekeeping, minding children for others is surely a great work. It is at the heart of life. Yet this is not always noticed or recognised. We need a St Zita. She gave her whole life to a family – housekeeping, minding children for others. Zita used to say that "work-shy piety is sham piety". She was not always popular with her companion workers. But her heart was in the right place. I imagine that Zita's secret was in listening more than in managing. Many parents today are drawn between two loves – giving precious time to their children and finding money to give a reasonable standard of life for their children. They need our encouragement and support.

28 APRIL

Peter Chanel – France – 19th century

You'll never walk alone, the song says. But true conscience at times has to walk alone as Jesus Christ did. Church and state want to make a better world. They link arms in that direction, but there can be tension about what 'better world' means. Religion is about here and hereafter. Politics is about here and here, Father Colm Kilcoyne says. Religion seeks a better world in respect for the person and our environment because of God's love. Peter Chanel chose a lonely road to walk as a missionary in Oceania on the island of Futuna in the New Hebrides. He endeared himself to the people, learning their language, adapting to their way of life. When the chief's son on the island requested Christian baptism, the chief became alarmed and had Peter murdered. Later, because of this tragedy, the whole island became Christian.

29 APRIL

Catherine of Siena – Italy – 14th century

Catherine is a fascinating person. A twenty-fourth child. In her teens she cut off her beautiful hair to avoid the attention of the boys and the prospect of marriage. Although almost illiterate she became a brilliant mind and an astute advisor. While her heart was with the poor and with the sick, she challenged Popes and princes. She went to Avignon and persuaded the exiled Pope Gregory XI to return to Rome. She stayed in Rome for six years to encourage and castigate his successor, Pope Urban VI. She died at the age of 33. Here are some of her treasured words: "Don't think of past sins except in the light of infinite mercy. Trust the Saviour's mercy." "Neither virtue or merit consist in penances or bodily excesses." "Merit consists in the virtue of love alone, flavoured by true discretion." She prayed: "O God, you are in love with the beauty of your creature, because you are gentle and without trace of bitterness, O eternal Trinity."

30 APRIL

Pius 5th – Italy – 16th century

There is the law of love and there is the love of law. It is a delicate balance. The Christian God puts love first because we have to be born before we can breathe or act. Having said that, we need the laws of the institution, the framework and scaffolding, to express love. We need home rules for basic harmony and peace, to avoid chaos. Pius V, although saintly, was a love of law man who tried to reform the post-Trent Church and his chaotic world. He saw the Protestants of his day and the Turks as enemies to be fought, if not destroyed. John XXIII, also saintly, was a law of love man, also trying to reform his chaotic world of the twentieth century. He saw all humanity as one family, full of different religions and persuasions, but all brothers and sisters; all at one in our pain, in our struggles and in our suffering. For him there must be no war, no condemnations. The great peacemaker of our time, he hugged all humanity, warts, wounds and all. The true spirit of love makes us free, St Paul says, because it is patient and kind, not jealous or boastful, envious or rude, but compassionate and generous.

May

1 MAY

Joseph – Palestine. 1st century

Joseph was chosen by God to protect his plan for humanity when it would be at its most vulnerable. Oh, to have this vote of confidence! It is easy to miss the character of the man Joseph. In innocence he suffered the depths of loneliness, but his trust in God saved the nations and reconciled his family. Joseph keeps his loyalty to Mary despite the odds of suspicion and fear. His God is the compassionate Father whose name is mercy. Joseph is worker and provider. Love is tested through the commitment of life, the everyday routine of job and survival and the limitations of our own make up. Love includes emotion, but it is more than emotion. Love is about decision making. Joseph had difficult decisions to face for his family's survival.

2 MAY

Athanasius – Alexandria – 4th century

The trees are in suspense, waiting with intense anxiety for the word, that in the beginning, first stirred the dark branch tree of humanity. Patrick Kavanagh, the Irish poet, had no problems linking the human and the divine. God is transcendent, but touches all creation and humanity through his Word, Jesus Christ, who became flesh and dwelt amongst us. It seems that many emperors in the days of Athanasius, with the help of the priest Arius, preferred to confine God to his transcendent, authoritarian place in Heaven. This made life easier for them and guaranteed their own power more effectively. The idea of a God of love and suffering in Jesus Christ, did not help their mission. But Athanasius stood in the gap and devoted his life to the defence of Jesus as divine, not just an exalted creature. "The word of God, incorruptible, came down to our world, not that he had been far off before. No part of creation was ever without him. Together with his Father he filled all things. He came full of love for us and took pity on our weakness." St Teresa of Avila says that the great flaw of the Christian is to think that God is absent (far away, outside life, in his heaven). We thank Athanasius for the God of pots and pans, bits and pieces, twists and turns, that make up our human lives.

3 MAY

Philip – Galilee – 1st century

Philip was one of the chosen twelve companions of Jesus. He was a good listener, but also a good question and answer man. "Where will we get bread to feed these hungry people?" he asks. Philip is blunt – "Send them home." Jesus speaks of the wonder of the Father's love. Philip says, "Show us this Father". "Have I been so long with you, Philip, and you don't know me," says Jesus. "Seeing me is seeing the Father." "Come see" are Philip's words and he must have learned them from Jesus. God always invites his children, come and see. He does not force. When we see God's love the heart is moved to renew the world with loving concern.

4 MAY

Gothard – Bavaria – 10th century

The Gothard Pass links Switzerland and Italy in a wonderful world of mountain, sky and fresh air. Gothard built a church there and provided a hospice for travellers. He was a practical man who translated his love of God into care and concern for everyday people. God does not force or command us, but God's way is love. Love is expressive and cannot be confined or kept to oneself. Love is social. You are my friends.

5 MAY

Edmond Rice – Ireland – 19th century

The Penal Laws in Ireland deprived Catholic people of property and freedom. Edmond Rice set out to educate the deprived young boys who were roaming the streets and quayside in Waterford. He sold his business and set up the first school in a converted stable in New Street, Waterford in 1802. At Mount Sion he built a Bake House that would provide food for hungry schoolchildren. He organised a Tailor's Shop that would give clothes to those who were cold and underprivileged. He made his way to Dublin City and began a first school in a large shed. This was the beginning of many schools. The legendary patriot Patrick Pearse was a pupil of this school. Edmond Rice was a friend of Daniel O'Connell. He befriended and helped Carlo Bianconi to begin his original transport system in Ireland. The Brothers and Edmond

Rice brought the enlightenment of education to millions throughout the world – Ireland, England, New South Wales, India, North America and South Africa. The dignity and well-being of the human person were at the centre of Edmond's idea of education. It was inspired by the Good News of Jesus Christ – the Glory of God.

6 MAY

Dominic Savio – Italy – 19th century

Tiger Woods made world history by winning the Masters Golf Classic in the USA. He was the youngest-ever winner and a black man. It was not so much his winning as the manner of his winning that was impressive. He had perfected every aspect of his game. He was good-humoured, gracious and courteous, in a way that belied his years. Dominic Savio was a teenage saint. Those who knew him said he had a knowledge of people in need and a great awareness of the spiritual needs of those around him. Perhaps we underestimate the spiritual qualities of young people, their enthusiasm in different areas of life: song, dance and games; the loyalty of their friendships, their concern for the environment and the hungry of this world.

7 MAY

John of Beverley – England – 8th century

John of Beverley must have been a very busy man. He went to school in Canterbury, joined the Benedictines in Whitby, became Bishop of Hexham and Archbishop of York. He died in Beverley Monastery. It is said that he loved roaming in the woods. The feel of God's intimate presence was there. We – our spirit – needs time to look at the flowers, to roam in the woods, to feel the unknown God in whom we live, move and have our being, through Jesus Christ.

8 MAY

Julian of Norwich – England – 14th century

Life's anxieties can overthrow the mind. We are left speechless in the presence of suicide. We can feel a sense of blame and "if only". It is a pain that somehow is reflected in the mental anguish of Jesus Christ who prayed, "My God, why have you forsaken me?" Julian of Norwich was restless as a young person. She often prayed for an illness which would draw her closer to God. Yet without her endurance and trust in life, we would have been deprived of her words of wisdom:

"All shall be well and all manner of things shall be well. All life is in the care of the Father and on its way to the Father. Life is like a river running to the ocean. We are asked to trust ourselves with the water like leaves on a stream. Because we exist we are carried home. His eye is on the sparrow and I know he is watching me – lovingly."

9 MAY

Peter Nolasco – France – 13th century

There is worry about drug abuse today. Young people can wreck their lives through drug addiction. Victims and pushers need release from a living death. Peter of Nolasco volunteered to give his life to ransom others who were slaves to death during the Moorish conquest of Spain. His ransom mission was blessed by the Bishop of Barcelona in 1223. His method was prayerful trust in God, and even the giving of himself as an exchange hostage. Helping to make the home a place of unconditional love, where young people are encouraged to express ideas and be listened to is one of the best safeguards against addiction. It is wise to have an understanding and informed mind about drugs, to have basic home rules with boundaries, to welcome our children's friends, to know their whereabouts outside home, to realise that there are helps in times of difficulty.

10 MAY

Antonino – Italy – 15th century

We had to learn things by heart at school, especially catechism, prayers and poetry. It is now called memorisation. It was often many years before the memorised words bore fruit. A prayer or a poem revisited in adult life can become heartfelt through reflection. Antonino was 15 years old when he memorised a book of canon law called the *Decretals of Gratain*. It was the price he had to pay for entering religious life. We have good memories and bad memories. Prayer and poetry can heal the bad memories and make us grateful for the good memories.

11 MAY

Francis di Girolamo – Italy – 17th century

Jesus Christ was criticised for the company he kept. He was friendly with prostitutes and sinners and ate with them. They would not have accepted him unless he spoke their language. I imagine that Jesus always saw good in every person. He was far-seeing. He saw the possibilities in every human heart, maybe not flowering today, but blooming later. Francis di Girolamo was a priest much loved by the people of Naples. Prisons, brothels, pawn shops, street corners were the places where he met friends. There is good in the worst of us and bad in the best of us, and it ill behoves the best to criticise the worst.

12 MAY

St Pancras – Rome – 4th century

I wonder what Pancras the teenage martyr in Rome would think of his St Pancras borough in London today, with its hospitals, railway systems, underground travel, churches, shops, buildings, hotels. It is a meeting place of the world. The ripples from the young Pancras' life have somehow touched our lives 2000 years on. Such is the marvel of what we are privileged to do in life. The impact of our being and action, in God's providence, is garnered down the centuries, like the giving of parents, the work of builder and artist, the people behind the scenes, the everyday simple jobs, answering calls, cleaning up, keeping the world. Nothing is lost. Reviewing the Kingdom will be very exciting.

13 MAY

Our Lady of Fatima – Portugal – 20th century

"He had great faith in the rosary ring you gave him in hospital", his widow said. "It was a friend to the end – a lifeline." The rosary ring is a ten-bead circle for the finger, that helps us to say a Hail Mary or reminds us of Mary. Often we don't know how to pray – what to say. We have little religious inclination. Yet we feel the need of help. The wonder of the Hail Mary is, that Mary does the praying for us. "Holy Mary, pray for us now." She interprets our needs, speaking for us. The little children of Fatima believed that The Lady asked them to pray the rosary for peace in the world. The rosary is a way of contemplation, because it focuses on the important events in the life of Jesus that tell of God's love. The rosary is the lay person's bible, but also a companion through the sadness, joys and hopes of life. It does not tie us to numbers or time. We can say fifteen decades or say a half a Hail Mary as we walk or wait.

14 MAY

Matthias – Palestine – 1st century

The Holy Book says, "The lot fell on Matthias." The lot was the vacant mission left over after Judas' departure. I wonder how Matthias felt about his new appointment. Often it is our weak points that precede us into new jobs. People can be over-cautious about us, ultra-suspicious. One remembers always the person who welcomes and risks being a friend in the new cool climate of a different working world. The friend in need is the friend indeed. The old wisdom said: in a new appointment change nothing for six months, observe, and avoid hankering back nostalgically to the last job. Going back is non-productive. Opportunity knocks in the new situation, and light creeps in when we realise we can only change ourselves, not others.

15 MAY

Isidore – Madrid – 12th century

Isidore is the saint of Madrid. Goya, the famous Spanish artist, popularised his memory. He was a farm worker. He loved the earth and respected the soil. The earth is our mother that sustains us unconditionally, endlessly and almost silently. I admire the spirituality of people, especially young people, who are concerned about our environment, who are sensitive to pollution and litter and destructive armaments. Through him all things were made and not a single thing was made without him. We are not owners of creation for exploitation, we are stewards of creation for co-operation.

16 MAY

John Nepomucen – Bohemia – 14th century

John Nepomucen is a familiar name in the city of Prague. He is said to have refused to reveal the confessional secrets of the Queen. King Wenceslaus IV had him pay the price with his life. We are called to love in different ways. One way is to be loyal to a friend in keeping a secret. Another can be to tell the secret if people's lives are being endangered, or if harm can be avoided. The choice can be very lonely. We need God's help. We can also be the stewards of God's help, through honestly given advice to another and through passing on the words of Jesus in the Gospel.

17 MAY

Paschal Baylon – Spain – 16th century

The month of May is First Communion time in many places throughout the world. First Communion celebrates the wonder of a child, and the wonder of God's assurance to us – You are my friends. It is a time to remember and to say thanks. To say thanks is the best gift of a human being. We celebrate thanks at church. Paschal Baylon spent hours praying in the presence of the Blessed Sacrament. His thanks were expressed in his everyday duty of door-keeping. We are always being called to open doors or answer phones for others in the different duties of life. The Jesus of our First Communion shows us the way to open the heart, and gives us his spirit not to lose heart.

18 MAY

John 1st – Italy – 6th century

Blessed are the peacemakers. Peacemakers are like parents with children. There is involvement, understanding, tolerance, respect for individuality, but also leadership and discipline. It is a risk-taking mission. It is much easier to be a peace lover, sitting on the sideline, wishing the world was a better place, but doing nothing about it. It is better to light a candle than to curse the darkness. John I did not want to be Pope, neither did he want to go to Constantinople to the emperor on a peacemaking mission. He pleaded with the emperor to allow Arian churches to be reopened, but refused to ask the emperor to let converts go back to their Arian beliefs. Theoderic, the local king, was suspicious and thought that John had done a deal with the Emperor against him, so he kidnapped him and had him imprisoned in Ravenna.

19 MAY

Felix of Cantalice – Italy – 16th century

Don't expect thanks, I was once advised, and if it happens it's a "perk". Often people we do most for, seem the least appreciative. But it must not dishearten nor embitter us. We have an opportunity to help. This is a privilege. The greatest gift of a human being is to say thanks. Felix was nicknamed the "Thank you" Brother. He was always saying "Thanks be to God." He had a sense of humour too. During carnival time he dressed up another Brother like Jesus and with a rope around his neck led him to the carnival. He made up songs to sing with the children. His idea of life was to look up, not down. Every creature in the world will raise our hearts to God if we look up with a good eye.

20 MAY

Bernardine of Siena – Italy – 15th century

In the world of communication the spoken word only counts for nine per cent impact. Body language and other factors make up 93 per cent. Bernardine lived at a time like that of the Chernobyl disaster. Twenty people a day were dying of the Black Death. Bernardine devolved his time and energy caring for the sick. He was the world's greatest preacher, yet he had a throat ailment and a hoarse voice. He spoke strongly against the abuse of gambling. As a result a businessman lost his card trade. Bernardine suggested that he should start making cards with IHS on them, meaning the name of Jesus. It was a sell-out success. The power of the love of Jesus in his heart influenced all his actions and words. He touched every aspect of life and living. He was fiery and funny.

21 MAY

Sillaeus – Italy – 12th century

Money creeps into everything, they say. An Irish bishop, son of St Brendan, wandered into the town of Lucca, Italy. He made a big impact, died there and was acclaimed a miracle worker. When a local chief demanded money from the convent where his remains were revered, the flow of cures suddenly stopped. There is an Irish tradition that says, "There is no fee for a cure, but you give a voluntary gift." It is a good instinct because all gifts are given, all is on loan, so let's not get greedy.

22 MAY

Rita of Cascia – Italy – 15th century

Rita was married against her will to a drunken partner. He was murdered. Her two sons wanted to avenge his death, but they died prematurely – an answer to her prayer. Rita is called The Saint of the Impossible. She ranks with St Jude (Hopeless Cases) on the popularity charts. She tells that God always hears our prayer and gives us what we need, but not always what we want. A good prayer is not so much asking to avoid trial and difficulty, as asking to get through and cope with the hurdles and obstacles of life with God's help.

23 MAY

John Baptist de Rossi – Italy – 18th century

Celebrating the Sacrament of Forgiveness is now a joyful duty. The chief focus is on God's goodness and compassionate mercy – thank you God for loving me. There is not a preoccupation with the confessing – the call is: help me to live like Jesus and not to sin again.

John Baptist de Rossi enjoyed meeting farmers and traders in the marketplace by day and living with the homeless and displaced at night. He did not want to hear confessions. But the local bishop forced his arm into celebrating the Sacrament of Forgiveness. He became one of the greatest confessors the world had known. So we never know, do we?

24 MAY

Vincent of Lerins – France – 5th century

Vincent wrote these words of wisdom: "Let there be unity in essentials, liberty in doubtful matters, charity in all things." Sometimes we let ourselves get over-fussed about non-essentials, even in religion. We can get over-concerned about the ways of expressing religion, rather than focusing on the basics that God is Father and good and that we ought to care for one another. What colour is God's skin, the song asks? Every human colour, is the answer. The essential needs of life today are air and food and water, the blessing of a friend, God's light that we may see.

25 MAY

Bede – England – 8th century

The name Bede speaks of learning, scholarship and Christian faith. It is said that he was always writing, always praying, always reading, always teaching. Almost all his life was spent within the monastery walls. His favourite prayer was: "Glory be to the Father and to the Son and to the Holy Spirit." He had really taken the three names to heart. There is often good comfort in revisiting old prayers of childhood. We can find hidden treasures of wisdom and encouragement through the mist and dust of time. We are Trinity-made persons in the image of Father, Son and Spirit. We are earth-based, Heavenward-bound. That God exists as Trinity makes prayer varied. We worship the loving Father or Mother, the son Jesus with all the human touches of life and the Spirit who pervades all that exists, the breath of life in the daily round of the world.

26 MAY

Philip Neri – Italy – 16th century

I like celebrating ordination day on the feast of St Philip Neri. He was a great lover. He made people laugh. He only became a priest in later life. He liked singing and gathered people to sing together in the oratory in Rome. His favourite books were the Gospels and a book of jokes. He advised a gossipy person to throw a bag of feathers into the sky and then collect the scattered pieces.

The person complained that this would not be possible. Bad words about others are like scattered feathers, he said. It is difficult to stop the flow or collect the pieces, so be careful about injurious words. Say good words. His favourite prayer was, "Lord, keep your hand over Philip today or he will betray you."

27 MAY

Augustine – Italy – 7th century

One day a dog saw a rabbit. He gave chase, barking. Other dogs joined in the barking, but after a short time gave up the chase. One dog persevered in the challenge because he was the one that "saw" the rabbit. Jesus Christ saw the compassionate face of the Father turned towards all humanity – that inspired his mission. Augustine, in Rome, had a vision of bringing the Good News of God's Kingdom to far-away people in England. He wanted to abandon his mission soon after he set off, but Pope Gregory the Great persuaded him to persevere. So we have the great Cathedral of Canterbury today. The missionaries were received well by King Ethelbert in Kent. Augustine built a church and Benedictine Monastery at Canterbury. He had thousands of converts. His vision brought blessings to the world.

28 MAY

Germanus – France – 6th century

Germanus was nominated Bishop of Paris by the king. He was such a loveable man that the king fell under his influence. The king became very Christian in his care for the poor and underprivileged. Everything that concerned human beings was the concern of Germanus. He had a way with sinners. Like the Prodigal's Father he was not put off by human weakness and helplessness, but rather hugged sinful and broken humanity.

29 MAY

Maximinus of Triers – France – 4th century

The emperors of the west lived in Triers in 340. This was also the city of Maximinus. It was a hotbed of Arianism. Maximinus took on the challenge. He sheltered the great Athanasius. The Arians could not accept that Jesus was truly Son of God. Perhaps the Arian emperors of the east did not like the sound of a God in love with such wretched humanity. He was a threat to their image of authority and power. It suited these emperors to have a distant, judgmental and fearful God, but not the intimacy that Jesus taught. Sure, there is mystery, but more importantly there is the intimacy of God with humanity.

30 MAY

Joan of Arc – France – 15th century

Voices spoke to Joan of Arc and told her to rescue the city of Orleans from the English invader. She did rescue the city, but eventually she was captured and sold to the enemy and burnt at the stake as a witch and heretic in the marketplace of Rouen. The king asked her why he did not get voices, even though he was king. She said: "You do get voices, but you don't listen to them." Everything that exists has a voice. If a blade of grass, a grain of sand, a ray of light, a dancing shade could sing its song – what would it be? God speaks in the ordinary experiences of everyday life, through dark and light, tragedy and joy. We forget to pause a minute to reflect on our daily experiences and perhaps lack attentiveness when sharing our stories with others. In our dialogue with the things around us, we often fail to hear the word through which God would enlighten us.

31 MAY

Mary, Mother of Jesus – Palestine – 1st century

The little ones in First Communion class made fifteen coloured flags for the procession. Five were coloured green for hope; five were purple for sadness; five were yellow for happiness. Each flag had two words from the Good News of the Gospel story which caught a scene from the life of Jesus and Mary. The second green flag said: "Mary visits." Mary could not keep the good news of God's love to herself. She went to help Elizabeth, because her heart was bursting with joy. That is the real smell of a Christian person – wanting to serve others everyday, everywhere. Never meet a person without giving a gift, the spiritual man said. The gift of hello, the gift of a smile, the gift of a shake hands, the gift of noticing something to compliment, a style, a fashion, a fun idea, a joke.

June

1 JUNE

Justin – Palestine – 2nd century

Justin was a brilliant philosopher and a lay person. In his pursuit of truth he concluded that the Christian religion had the best answers to the mystery of life and death. He put his ideas in writing. The emperor felt threatened by his ideas and had him beheaded. Faith in Jesus Christ is a way of seeing. When we fall in love, what is ordinary – man, woman, cause, nature – becomes extraordinary. We are transformed. Our faces shine.

2 JUNE

Marcellinus and Peter – Italy – 4th century

Real humanity, wholesomeness, is when other people are thanked for things you do, and you can laugh. My friend founded a football club, gave it its name. It became very successful, but his name as first founder was never mentioned. Marcellinus and Peter banked on being unknown. They were beheaded for their Christian faith and secretly buried in the woods, but later one of the executioners became a Christian and two women rescued the remains from the woods and had them enshrined in the catacombs of Tiburtius in Rome. Later a basilica was built to their memory and Helena, mother of the Emperor Constantine, was buried with them. The ultimate integrity means doing the job as best as one can, irrespective of results. All that is good registers and counts.

3 JUNE

Kevin, Glendalough – Ireland – 7th century

A trip through the Wicklow Gap mountains to the lakes of Glendalough on a June day is a taste of heaven. Kevin made this place his heaven on earth. He was a soul friend of Ciaran of Clonmacnoise. Kevin's bed has been a place of pilgrimage for over a thousand years. The stones of Glendalough, the chattering waters of its streams, the silent lakes, the mountains framed in blue and white, whisper messages of immortal longing. Its vacancy is full of voices. A blind man sat on a stone playing a song on his musical instrument, he smiled at everyone although he saw no one.

4 JUNE

Francis of Caracciolo – Italy – 16th century

My hermit friend said that there are no accidents in God's providence. Even when bad things happen to good people, there is always a presence of God in the storm. Not that God ever sends evil or hurt, but he is present through it. An ordinary working priest, Francis, received an invitation one morning to participate in a new religious movement – helping condemned people to die. He felt complimented and turned up for the job, but alas it was a case of mistaken identity. The wrong man got the invitation. However, he decided to stay, took the name Francis and all worked out for good and even better.

5 JUNE

Boniface – England – 8th century

Boniface is patron of Germany. He was born in England and was christened Wynfrith. His heart's desire was to bring the Good News of God's love to the continent of Europe. He was an outstanding scholar and great organiser. Keeping basic order in family, school, church or state is never easy or popular. Yet without basic rules, particularly on the motorway, there would be chaos. Boniface saw commandments, not as restrictions, but as ways of loving God. Commandments are candle-lights of love that remind us of the Son, the ultimate fire of love.

6 JUNE

Norbert – Germany – 12th century

Lightning caused Norbert to fall off his horse. The accident changed his life. He devoted himself to people as a missionary. It was said that he was very charming and easy to talk to and he had the gift of appearing on equal terms with everyone. Thérèse of Lisieux advised her superior to try to make herself loveable, because then keeping God's rules would be easier for those in her care. A joyless religion is not the Christian religion, so better give it up. Such were the remarks of a friend celebrating the baptism of a child.

7 JUNE

Matt Talbot – Ireland – 20th century

Addiction of any kind strangles life. Drug abuse is a modern day addiction. The easy course, some say, is to keep the abusers and abused on the move. The more radical approach is to try to reform the person at source. Matt Talbot was an addict to drink. The worst, he said, was when he was refused drink in a pub because of his condition. He realised then that he had "gone to pot". He turned to God for help and strength, realising that he was too weak alone to break this chain of misery. He found the presence of God in the church and in the prayer of his heart. He beat the drink addiction and died peacefully. Love conquered. Parents worry about the ways and means of drugs and how to cope with their children. The best and first therapy is to love the person.

8 JUNE

Cecilia Caesarini – Italy – 13th century

I have been told that those who write should not, and those who don't, should. Cecilia was a nun in Dominic's convent. She wrote down words about Dominic that made exciting reading later on – that she admired his beautiful eyes, that the Sisters tried to get him to eat more and sleep on a proper bed, so that he would not be falling asleep during the day. Also noted was the fact that he would prefer to talk with young girls than to be talked at by old women. Also passed on to us were his nine ways of praying, how he talked to God through the gestures and attitude of the body. We are given hands to do our work, but also to stretch out like embracing branches to praise the Lord.

9 JUNE

Colmcille – Ireland – 6th century

Colmcille's spirit has touched every part of Ireland: Derry, Donegal, Durrow, Clonard, Kells, Swords, Longford, Glasnevin, Moone and many other places. He is also called Columba, which means dove. His flight brought him to found the great monastery of Iona in Scotland, whose Christian influence impacted throughout England and the continent. I imagine his leaving Ireland as a white martyrdom. Feeling restless one day I went to Durrow of Colmcille and its high cross. The winter sun was breaking through the outstretched tree branches, shedding light on this awesome place. Emerging spring-like daffodils spotlighted the humble surrounds, fields stretched far away towards the hills of Offaly. I felt restful and wanted to take its peace with me. I touched gently the face, side and base of the high cross, the Christ rock, and its beautiful ornamentation. I felt in touch with its artists and crafts persons and soothed by that faith of millions who have touched these stones and celebrated this place.

10 JUNE

Ephrem – Syria – 4th century

His name sings down through the centuries. It is said he pretended to be mad to avoid becoming a bishop. He wrote songs instead to praise God, and he wanted to avoid human praise. Ephrem wrote: "Lay me not with sweet spices, for this honour avails me not, nor yet use incense and perfumes, for the honour befits me not, escort me with your prayers. Give your incense to God. Over me send up songs. Be mindful of me, interceding mercy."

11 JUNE

Barnabas – Palestine – 1st century

The name means Son of Encouragement. He travelled with Paul and Mark, bringing the Good News message of Jesus Christ. He caught the spirit of Jesus' teaching – that God our Father is the God of all encouragement and kindness. The world longs for the word of encouragement, not threats of doom and gloom. The compassionate Father hugs our broken humanity. We don't need to be perfectly good or pure to earn his love. The Lord asks us to comfort one another with words of kindness and actions of generosity.

12 JUNE

Odulf – Holland – 9th century

Odulf was a popular, saintly man who lived in Belgium and Holland. His shrine was stolen by the Vikings and sold in London. It later found its way to Evesham Abbey. He was a man of all seasons. Perhaps he is reminding us today that love of God is greater than nationalism. God is larger than the boundaries of race or creed. God takes delight in all his people.

13 JUNE

Anthony of Padua – Portugal – 13th century

To someone who was asked to speak the teacher advised: "It is important to have something to say, rather than to say something." Anthony had something to say. The something was born from many experiences. As a young man he admired the five martyrs whose remains returned from Morocco. He went as a missionary to the Moors. He had poor health. His boat was driven off course and he landed in Sicily. He met St Francis and tried to hide his learning and talent by doing kitchen work. When asked to say a few words at an ordination, he stunned his audience with the excellence of his words and his winning personality. St Francis appointed him as teacher of theology. He is represented in art carrying the child Jesus in his arms. The words he spoke were words made flesh through the love of God and the care of people.

14 JUNE

Dogmael – Wales – 6th century

The only memory of Dogmael is that he helped children to learn to walk. Helping a child to walk is helping a person to grow in freedom and adventure. Once the children begin to walk, the mother said, they are running away from you. The desire of every parent is that their child will walk tall. If we analyse walking, we will notice that while one foot is firmly based on the ground, the other foot is off the ground – airborne. It is as if we walk on one foot while the other keeps the balance. To keep our human balance in life we need the mystery of something or someone other than ourselves that is outside and inside life.

15 JUNE

Germaine – France – 16th century

Germaine was born with a defective hand. She lost her mother in early life, felt rejected by her father and was ill-treated by her stepmother. She worked as a shepherdess. Her only book was the rosary, which she said everyday. She grew to love and help the local children, and found food for the poor. Her stepmother accused her of stealing bread and hiding it in her apron. When her apron was opened it was full of roses. The prayer "Holy Mary, pray for us now and at the hour of our death" was a lifeline for her. Often we don't know how to pray or what to say, but Mary prays for us. She knows our needs. She knows what is best for us.

16 JUNE

Lutgardis – France – 13th century

Bloom where you are planted is easier said than done. Lutgardis was dumped in a convent at twelve years of age because her parents did not have dowry money for her marriage. In time Lutgardis took to the religious life, found her call and peace of mind. Many people don't find life meaningful. They feel caught, if not dumped, in job situations, in marriage relationships – square pegs in round holes. People struggle to work for a living, pay the mortgage, and such are the poor the Lord has called blessed.

17 JUNE

Theresa of Portugal – 13th century

He said, "We have tried everything to save the marriage." She said, "Our love is dead. It was a mistake at the beginning. We owe it to ourselves, and to our children to separate. We intend to work out an arrangement amicably, without bitterness." Theresa of Portugal was happily married when the law decided that her marriage to her cousin was invalid. Alfonso took another woman, Beringeria. Theresa went into religious life. Inheritance rights for the children became a problem years later. Beringeria approached Theresa for help. Theresa willingly co-operated, without bitterness. Often in life we carry imaginary burdens, thinking that we have been snubbed, passed over, forgotten, when often the people we accuse don't even know or have never intended any hurt. Jesus says: "Don't carry enmity in your heart, it is an unnecessary burden wearing you down. Walk free and forgive."

18 JUNE

Elizabeth of Schonau – Germany – 12th century

When we think that we have been passed over and forgotten, when others get the praise, there is an answer to our problem. Jesus says: "Your Father who sees all that is done in secret, rewards you." He said this three times relating to fasting, prayer and what we give. When we try to do because it is right, rather than because of what people will say, it brings its own peace. All is for God's sake. Elizabeth of Schonau should have been passed over and forgotten because in her poverty she took refuge in a convent at the age of 12. She shared some of her prayer experiences with her brother who put them in writing. The people acclaimed her as a saint.

19 JUNE

Romuald, Italy – 10th century

Some people look at a garden and see only weeds – they miss the flowers. The providence of God assures us that flowers are there. God tells us that despite the desperate and tragic happenings of the world, light lurks in darkness, there is hidden hope and blessing, the sun behind the clouds. It is the light that makes shadows. Romuald became one of the greatest spiritual influences the world has known. He was a reformer, but not before he reformed himself. He saw his father murder a relative in a quarrel. This experience changed his life; he turned a new page and gave himself to the things of God.

20 JUNE

Silverius, Italy – 6th century

Pope Silverius is regarded as a martyr. It interests me that his father was Pope Hormisdas. The Empress Theodora did not like Silverius and made her presence felt. Today a Pope with a child and a woman murdering the Pope would raise our modern eyebrows, but God is full of surprises. Often it is the foolish and weak things that God uses in our own lives and in world events for his good purpose, as if to remind us that all fruitfulness is from God. We are always unprofitable servants. I am reminded of a friend whose comment in every unusual and tragic happening is always "how interesting" – never, "how terrible".

21 JUNE

Aloysius of Gonzaga – Italy – 16th century

There are horses for saddles and horses for straddles. Some for the glamour parade – some for the ordinary slogging of life. Aloysius was a kind of parade saint with his extraordinary penances. When he joined the Jesuits they showed him another way – putting up with others, coping with the unexpected happenings. Which is a greater poverty a lack of things, or a lack of privacy and letting people disturb our plans? Minding children is a great education, a poverty, with endless demands. Time is not one's own, worries are daily, there is the constant intrusion on one's privacy, through sleepless nights, health concerns, school problems, money necessities. I forget who said that parents are excused from prayer, because their lives are a prayer.

22 JUNE

Thomas More – England – 16th century

Thomas is called a Man for all Seasons: intelligent, witty, a family man, but above all a man of conscience. He clashed with Henry VIII on a question of conscience – what is right. He was beheaded in the Tower of London. To the judges who condemned him he said: "May we all meet merrily in Heaven. To the crowd he said: "I am the King's good servant, but God's first." At the executioner's block he asked: "May I take my beard out of the way, because it has committed no offence?"

23 JUNE

Etheldreda – England – 7th century

Etheldreda was married twice in unusual circumstances. But her marriages were never consummated. She decided to found a monastery in Ely. People find fulfilment in different ways in life. A psychiatrist said that the secret of success in marriage is being able to travel alone. It is unreal to expect a partner to make one happy. Happiness comes from inside one's self – it is not found in possession of a person or things. Joy is being used for a purpose, recognised by oneself as a mighty one.

24 JUNE

John the Baptist – Palestine – 1st century

The Spanish artist Murillo painted a picture of John the Baptist as a young child of curly hair, with his arms around a pet lamb. They are cheek to cheek in friendship, and the lamb stretches his front leg onto the arm of John in an affectionate gesture of intimacy. The setting is a dark landscape, with threatening clouds and slight rays of light. Murillo is expressing the innocent, almost shy and hidden love of God – the Lamb of God – which is guaranteed to us despite the dark sadness of the world, and the threatening fears of life. God's love is a pervasive love that embraces John, you and me, the environment we live in, the animal world. John's mission in life was to point us towards this unbelievable love.

25 JUNE

William of Vercelli – Italy – 12th century

William seemed fond of doing pilgrimages. He had his heart set on going to Jerusalem. He was attacked by robbers on the way and never made it. He founded a monastery on a mountain and there found his peace. Mother Teresa of Calcutta was once asked what was she doing for the 20,000 other poor children that were dying every day. She said: "God asked me to be faithful, not successful." If it happens, well and good, but the Christian way is not success and competition. It is compassion and co-operation. The daily faithful round of family life, work and survival.

26 JUNE

Anthelm – France – 12th century

Anthelm was a priest, a monk, a builder, a farmer, a reformer and a peacemaker. He believed that life is for living, not for keeping in cold storage. If rules depress us and squeeze the life out of us we are going the wrong way. Be life givers, Jesus said. Is what I do life giving or a kiss of death? He touches the untouchables, brought them in from the cold of rejection and discrimination. Of course I want to give you life, he said, as he touched the leper who was rejected because of his rotting humanity and poverty.

27 JUNE

Cyril of Alexandria – Egypt – 5th century

Cyril was a great friend, but a difficult enemy. He did not tolerate fools gladly, but he had an eagle eye for truth. Mary is not just the mother of the humanity of Christ, he said, she is truly God-bearer, mother of Jesus, real God and real man, our Saviour and our hope. Perhaps it was the manner in which he engaged his theological foes, the Nestorians, that raised their skin. People do desperate things to themselves and to others. We call each other all kinds of names from the animal kingdom, yet we are forever human beings, loveable – street angels and home devils. We can only change ourselves. We have to bear the pain of what we cannot change, and this is redemptive for the world.

28 JUNE

Irenaeus – Smyrna – 2nd century

A man arrived at Heaven's gate with two fistfuls of soil. He loved the earth so much that he could not part with it. Peter welcomed him and explained that Heaven was no problem. The only requisite was open hands, because God wants to shake hands and welcome us. But a closed fist cannot shake hands. Irenaeus got this kind of idea of God from John, who was Jesus' friend. God's love and mercy are for every single person, not earned. All we need is open hands. There were teachers in Irenaeus' day who wanted to reserve God's Heaven and God's love to the few, an elite, but Irenaeus fought bravely for us against that teaching. Here are some of his words of wisdom: "The Word, Jesus, and the Holy Spirit, are the two hands of the Father: with them he creates, directs, attracts, fulfils all humanity." "Christ was united to his own creation." "The Word never ceases coming down to humanity."

29 JUNE

Peter and Paul – Palestine – 1st century

Peter denied Jesus. Paul persecuted Jesus. Yet both were chosen as messengers of God's love. Peter is the parent in God's family. There have to be basic rules in family life, otherwise there is chaos. Rules are often misunderstood. They are meant for life and life-giving. Peter rules with love the people of God. Paul is a fire, a lover of humanity. He is intoxicated by the unbelievable love of God for all his people. He is not interested in laws; he is absorbed in the spirit of the law. That is love. God loves us all the time. Paul says, "Love is patient, kind, wants the good. Such is God." He said, "To me to live is Christ. I glory in my weakness because it is an opening for God to love me more."

30 JUNE

Pierre Toussaint – Haiti – 19th century

I remember making a score at a ball game once. But with bad press, another player got the honour for my score. It pinched hard. Pierre was a slave to the Berand landlords in Haiti. The Berand family introduced Pierre to the hairdressing business with a reputable client. Things went bad for the Berand, with debts and loss of property. Meantime, Pierre became very wealthy through the hairdressing business and now it was he who provided the necessities of life for Lady Berand. Yet he continued to serve at her table, hiding the real truth of her deprivation. When she was dying she granted Pierre his freedom. Paul sows. Apollo waters. God gives the increase. Somehow great human people are so focused on God as love, and giving all, that they see their sowing and watering in life as a privilege, not a need for applause.

July

1 JULY

Oliver Plunkett – Ireland – 17th century

As I walked in pilgrimage from London Tower to Tyburn, I thought of Oliver Plunkett making his last journey – to be hanged, drawn and quartered for conscience and truth. He was the last of the martyrs of the faith to die at Tyburn. A Protestant court refused to condemn him in Dundalk, Ireland. But there were other enemies among his own people. When he was asked by Pope Clement to leave Rome and go as pastor to a troubled Ireland, he knew the fate of his predecessors – one died at the Tower of London. Another was murdered at Tulsk and five others died in exile. His was an extraordinary love to face such a storm. He died without bitterness for king or accusers. Coping with the unlovable bits in others means pain and suffering. Jesus accepted it. So did Oliver Plunkett, and made it redemptive.

2 JULY

Junipero Serra – Spain – 18th century

There is a highway in California called the Juniperoserra. It is appropriately named. Junipero Serra was a Franciscan Brother who founded nine Catholic missions in California. He was a phenomenal walker. The cities and towns with the prefix "San" recall his memory along the Californian coast. The song says: "If I can love somebody, as I walk along, then my living shall not be in vain." Walking makes it easier to have an eye for people, to give attention to what's around. In the car or jogging, I cannot relish in the same way the children playing, babies wandering, dogs walking, the birds' air display, their songs, the other person's garden, the different flowers, the shape of houses, the trees, the clouds, the mountains, the sunshine. It is good to walk.

3 JULY

Thomas – Palestine – 1st century

A priest was very sensitive about the media comments on the Church, and felt somewhat ashamed and embarrassed. An old man said to him: "Well, the Good Lord was crucified in the company of two thieves and he didn't object or get too fussy." We need an eye of faith to see through the wounds to the beauty. That is oneself, or the people who surround our lives in all their wounds and weaknesses. The Prodigal's Father was not put off by sin, impurity and dishonesty. We long for and need a St Thomas Conversion. He was invited to see through the hands of the wounds, to see them as the window of the Christ. He could only say: "My Lord and my God."

4 JULY

Elizabeth of Portugal – 13th century.

Blessed are the peacemakers. We all love peace, but really human people make peace. Elizabeth of Portugal was a real peacemaker. She stopped a battle between her husband the king and her son Alfonso. She prevented a war between Portugal and Castile. She had a difficult and varied life, but she found the God of peace in its midst.

5 JULY

Antony Zaccaria – Italy – 16th century

Antony's father died when he was young. He became a doctor. Through the compassion of his mother he became very sensitive to the poor and street people. He became a priest and chose the streets of Milan for his mission. He gathered groups around him to extend this mission of compassion. Jesus tells and shows that the Father's way is compassion. Lucy nurses her ailing husband lovingly. His mind is failing. There are moments when he can become quite violent and a threat to himself and others. She tells me: "That's not really him, it's the illness." This is a taste of Heaven, a meeting with God who can only see us with love.

6 JULY

Maria Goretti – Italy – 19th century

Maria was murdered by a young man, Alessandro, in a rage of passion. Alessandro served 27 years in prison for his crime. He said that Maria used to appear to him in a dream, holding white lilies. Alessandro and Maria's mother celebrated together Maria's canonisation in Rome in 1950. Alessandro had asked the mother for forgiveness, and he had been granted forgiveness. Sometimes we feel that an eye for an eye and a tooth for a tooth is the right way. Jesus walking this earth offered a better way. There is always more to us in God's eye than we can see. There is the harmful heat of passion, but there is also the passion that makes a wonderful world of children and families and relationships and grandparents. So don't carry a baggage of bitterness in your heart.

7 JULY

Pier Giorgio Frassati – Italy – 20th century

Pat was totally paralysed with polio, except for her head and face. She lived in a coffin-like box, that breathed for her. She learned to type by using her lips to blow into a complicated machine. She wrote me her first letter, which I still cherish. She said that every day you awaken, you have to adjust yourself again to your position. You never realise how wonderful it is to be able to feed yourself, to chose the bits you like to eat. It is never the same being fed. It is exhilarating to be able to comb your own hair, wash your face, wipe your brow. There are the boring visitors who are curious and the welcome visitors who tell you about their life and what's going on. Blessed Pier Giorgio Frassati died of polio at the age of 24. He too, like Pat, was a mountain climber, young and beautiful. I don't know if he had long black hair like her. But he loved life, style, theatre, art, personalities and a cigar.

8 JULY

Rose Hawthorne Lathrop – USA – 20th century

When Rose's husband died, she began to work with cancer patients and she gathered a group of Sisters to help her in this work. Over and above the necessities of life, she tried to find out the particular interest of a patient, maybe a pet dog, a cat, a bird, a flower, an author, a poet, a song. Sometimes we can be so religious that we miss the human, the ordinary, what makes the person tick and be different. The last time I was a patient in hospital, I remember getting a Lotto card. I got joy rubbing off the silver lining to find, once again, that I had not won a fortune.

9 JULY

Nicholas Piech and companions – Holland – 16th century

Nineteen priests and religious were hanged for their religious beliefs in Gorkum, Holland, during the Reformation. Many people can be saddened because of the terrible inhumanities perpetrated in the name of religion. It is true, no religion is better than bad religion. Jesus Christ was against every kind of discrimination when he walked this earth. Good Pope John XXIII asked the world to search for what we have in common. All our blood is red, we long to be loved, colour of pain and sickness is the same for all, we need mother earth to sustain us, we can only eat one meal at a time, wear one suit of clothes. It is important to be sensitive to careless remarks we make about other people's traditions, their religious culture or practice. Let's not say about another what we would not like to hear about ourselves.

10 JULY

Theodosius – Russia – 11th century

He opted out of a well-to-do family and became a labourer in the fields. He trained as a baker, before becoming a monk. He was a moderate. He encouraged his monks to build the Kingdom of God on this earth by being involved in the ordinary affairs of the day and in the lives of people. He set up hostels and hospitals. Like Thérèse of Lisieux he was a saint for our times. She saw the everyday happenings, the people we have to cope with, and the accidents of life as petals, put in our hands by a loving "Rose" God. If we trust the all-loving Father, it does not matter what befalls. Madelaine had a very disturbed family background. She suffered much abuse, which affected her confidence and made her fearful and unattractive. Thérèse tells her that it is the way we respond to all that happens that is vital, not what happens to us, no matter how shameful. We have to allow ourselves to be children again, shadows and all, carried by God's love.

11 JULY

Benedict – Italy – 6th century

Subiaco and Monte Cassino are places of wonder. Benedict, like the Celtic monks, chose the most beautiful locations in the world for his life of prayer and solitude. There was a particular presence of God in the mountain and lake, in river and valley, island and inland. All is a touch of the Master's hand. The great appeal of Benedict was his moderation. He caught the balance between work and prayer. For him, Martha, the activist, and Mary, the contemplative, are the same person. His rule of love was challenging for the big-hearted and generous, but encouraging for the weak ones. There is a joy in knowing that we are carried by God's love, as a parent carries a little child. The child does not have to prove its worth. Religion that makes us fearful or sad does not come from the God of Benedict or Jesus Christ.

12 JULY

John Gualbert – Italy – 11th century

John was intent to kill the murderer of his brother, Hugo. He met the criminal. It was Good Friday. As John drew his sword, the culprit begged his mercy in honour of the Passion of Jesus Christ. John relented. He embraced his enemy and decided to enter the Order of St Benedict. Often we can feel weighed down by bitterness, and tortured by what we think are "enemies". A monk threw an old stick into a fresh, flowing stream. Soon it had disappeared. With the stick he threw away his bitterness, hate and anger. It was swallowed up and lost in the flowing stream of God's mercy.

13 JULY

Henry 2nd – Italy – 10th century

Henry was an active Emperor of Europe. He did battle for empire and Church. Yet he was a man of prayer. While returning from battle he prayed to Benedict in Monte Cassino. He was cured of illness, but it is said that he retained a limp. God calls us to bring life and love to our human situation. Whether single, married, religious, working for Church or State, we can participate in the plan of Jesus to bring life and love to the world. Sometimes the price may be getting a limp. Perhaps it is then we realise that we are carried by the compassionate Father all the time and we learn to trust more.

14 JULY

Camillus de Lellis – Italy – 16th century

Camillus was a big man in every sense. An uncontrollable gambler, bad-tempered and a fighting soldier, he had a diseased leg. During his depressions he took refuge in a Capuchin monastery. He heard a sermon one day that encouraged him to turn over a new leaf. He was twice rejected by the Capuchins for his bad leg. He decided to set up his own caring mission for the sick, especially prisoners, galley slaves, and the worst rejects. The field ambulance, during war, was his idea. It is our constant temptation to give up when our effort, or idea, or dream fails, or is set back first time. But often it can be just a postponed success. We were not ready at that time. Wine matures with the waiting. I could see my friend's talent for Montessori teaching. It was only after her work experience in Germany and the USA that she became committed to the Montessori dream and now has begun her own school.

15 JULY

Bonaventure – Italy – 13th century

St Francis of Assisi prayed good fortune for a sick child. So they called the child Bonaventure, which means "good fortune". He brought the spirit of St Francis to many troubled people. He was a healer of dissensions. He avoided honours and publicity. But he was obliged to become Cardinal Bishop of Albano. When the dignitaries arrived with his cardinal's hat, Bonaventure was washing dishes in the kitchen. He liked to say the Hail Mary every night, and ring a bell. Maturity, it is said, is being able to enjoy others being thanked for the jobs you did. Bonaventure felt privileged to do whatever job came his way, for its own sake. The rewarding joy is the privilege. He thanked God for using him.

16 JULY

Our Lady of Mount Carmel and Simon Stock – England – 13th century

A mother was explaining to her teenager that Our Lady had been very good to their family, protecting them from serious injury and harm, and that she should go to Mass on Our Lady's Feast Day. The teenager asked: "Does Our Lady then not protect those who have been injured or harmed?" The mother had to rethink her presentation on the role of Mary. Mary was not saved from hurt, shame, disappointment, rejection or tragedy herself. But she believed that God was always with her, loving her through the darkness. When bad things happen to good people, there is no explanation, but God is always with us, helping us through.

Simon Stock saw "The Black Scapular" as a sign of Our Lady's concern for all people. Mary prays for us always and at the hour of our death.

17 JULY

Martyrs of Compiegne – France – 18th century

Sixteen Carmelite nuns were expelled from their convent during the French Revolution. They spilt into four groups and decided to carry on their religious life, privately and prayerfully. They were arrested, imprisoned and condemned to death by the revolutionaries. They sang hymns as they went to their death. The astonished crowd remained silent. Violence breeds violence, rather than true freedom. True freedom is born from respect for human rights and life. Jesus did not use violence, although he suffered the effects of violence to redeem our humanity.

18 JULY

Bruno – Italy – 11th century

Bruno was a great scholar and a negotiator. He wanted to get away from it all. He resigned as bishop and went to the Monastery of Monte Cassino. But the people objected, and he was obliged to withdraw his resignation. He did, but remained in the monastery, until Pope Paschal forced him to return to his diocese. We get scattered and distressed by the many demands of life. We need a marker like Bruno to remind us that there is only one "me", unique, original, not to be possessed by any person or thing. We must make time to smell the flowers, to breathe the air and to listen to our heartbeat.

19 JULY

Arsenius – Italy – 4th century

I imagine Jesus instructing his friends to tell the people about the Father – the all-compassionate God. They keep asking him: "But what do we bring with us, how much money do we need, how many clothes, how much food?" Jesus says: "Take nothing, tell the Good News of the Father's love." Arsenius was weighed down with the splendour of his lifestyle. He decided to take to the desert, because all these things did not satisfy him. God knows we have to live with the things of life. Do the best for our children and our family. Money is food and blood. Yet the wise people of the world remind us to distinguish between our needs and our wants. Needs are basic. Wants can be a runaway horse of greed, good for neither body nor soul.

20 JULY

Justa and Rufina – Spain – 4th century

Justa and Rufina of Seville did beautiful pottery work with their hands, but they refused to have their gifts used for sacrifice to the Roman gods; so they were executed. It is said that if we don't pray to or relate to some other being greater than ourselves, we can fall into worshipping ourselves. This leads to madness. Humans are people who depend for life on love. It is a blessing to ask the compassionate Father, who knows our needs, and encourages us always to search because it is good for our sanity.

21 JULY

Lawrence of Brindisi – Italy – 16th century

It is strange to think of Lawrence of Brindisi, with a crucifix held aloft, leading an army to battle against the Turks. We cannot think of peacemaking people doing such things in the name of the Christian God who teaches non-violence. Lawrence's special blessing was, I think, his ability to learn many languages. This gave him access to the hearts and minds of many people, in many countries. It is always a compliment to another to speak his or her language. Jesus spoke the language of the ordinary people, otherwise they would not want to eat, drink and talk with him. I watched children of different languages and customs, playing together. Their communication was larger than language. The heart has its own language.

22 JULY

Mary Magdalene – Palestine – 1st century

A beautiful fifteenth-century painting shows Mary Magdalene sitting restfully on the ground, a perfume ointment jar by her side, and the book of God's word in her hands. She is beautiful, humble and graceful. She is not doing things. She is waiting, resting, not anxious about methods or ways of prayer. She is just there. The perfume jar suggests that real prayer expresses itself in wanting to pour healing oil on troubled people and use scented hands to give encouragement to the broken and distressed of this day.

23 JULY

Bridget of Sweden – 14th century

While Bridget was telling the worldly popes of Avignon and Rome what to do, her daughter Catherine was becoming a saint, and her son was becoming a renegade. What a remarkable woman. Married, with eight children, yet also she was foundress of two monasteries – one for men, the other for women – peacemaker, negotiator, mystical visionary. Yet she kept her feet steadily on the ground. In one of her visions God said to her: "Through the humanity I assumed, you are all my brothers and sisters, and as brothers and sisters I judge." The compassionate love of the Father is the bedrock of Christian faith.

24 JULY

Francis of Solano – Spain – 16th century

I wonder if Francis learned to play his violin on the streets of Granada to encourage plague-stricken people. When he emigrated to South America he had outstanding success as a missionary, among the Indians, in Peru, Argentina, Uruguay and Paraguay. He played the violin for them. I often wonder why learning a musical instrument was not compulsory in seminary training. Hours were spent on complicated abstractions, while the people we would meet and serve would long for a song, to distract them from their everyday worries. I imagine Francis singing: "Dance, dance, wherever you may be, I am the Lord of the dance, said he, and I'll lead you all wherever you may be, and I'll lead you all in the dance, said he."

25 JULY

Christopher

Christopher is an everyday saint. I like the Christopher medal to keep me company when driving the car. The word Christopher means Christ-bearer. Christopher is always represented as a strong man, carrying a child safely on his shoulders across a raging stream. It is said that when he became a Christian he took on that kind of "taxi service" for others. He reminds me that it is kind to give a lift to a fellow human being, even at risk. He also reminds me to drive the car with respect and courtesy for other human beings. So I ask myself today – "Did I watch that mirror to let others pass by? Did I honk that horn impatiently, or did I bear with the weakness of our humanity?"

26 JULY

Joachim and Ann – Palestine – 1st century

Joachim and Ann were the parents of Mary. Lorenzo Lotto paints a picture of the young grandparent, Ann, helping Mary with the Infant Jesus. Mary and the Child Jesus touch affectionately, and rest in the presence of Ann, almost enveloped in her cloak. Ann's hands are held in a kind of waiting gesture. I think of Ann as the patroness of grandparents. She is there in support, not taking over, or interfering too much, but always ready to help, maybe more by admiration and positive comments, than active work. The eyes of Ann are totally for her daughter and grandchild. Such grandparents are God's greatest blessing.

27 JULY

Nathalia and Aurelius – Spain – 8th century

Cordova today is a city that lives in harmony with its Christian, Jewish and Muslim traditions. Nathalia and Aurelius were husband and wife. They conformed to Muslim customs outwardly, but lived the Christian faith inwardly and secretly. Then they decided to go public. They were martyred. We often hear people say that religion is a private matter. Yet, if religious faith is about love, love cannot live in isolation. It needs to express itself. Perhaps the sadness of the agnostic is that he has nobody to thank when he is very happy. It is not fair to be a member of a family, but not play one's part to support the others. The Christian family person supports others through church celebration, with presence, prayer, financial support and friendship in God's name.

28 JULY

Pantaleon – Rome – 4th century

The name Pantaleon means "all compassion". When he became Christian he got the reputation of caring for the sick without pay. He surely caught the Good News of the Christian message. Jesus came to change our image of God, from someone remote and fearful, to the all-compassionate Father. He also came to change the image we have of ourselves: although we are disheartened by our imperfections, we are mischievous children that God wants to love. Thérèse of Lisieux said to God that she was too small, weak and inadequate to climb the stairs of perfection. Would he become her lift, take her in his arms in all her weakness and nothingness? God said yes, and she became a saint.

29 JULY

Martha – Palestine – 1st century

I gave a dinner for my friends. Thinking of their likes and dislikes made me work imaginatively for several days. I tried, at mealtime, to keep an eye on my company – which meant movement and activity. Halfway through the meal my good friend said: "For God's sake, will you sit down and talk with us – that's more important than food." The episode disposed me forever in favour of "the Martha's" of this world, who have to plan and prepare meals and hold celebrations of all kinds. I don't believe that Martha's guest said: "You fuss too much." I think Jesus was really saying: "I'd love your company. Don't deprive me." When we like ourselves, as God likes us, we will feel secure, to take that break, to leave the washing, the beds and the dusting and the garden until tomorrow.

30 JULY

Peter Chrysologus – Italy – 5th century

If you don't strike oil in the first minute, stop boring. That was advice to a preacher. People say that sermons are too long, too boring and out of touch with reality. Then why do we persist? Are the people out of touch with reality, or is it that some preachers are? I still remember with joy the priest who said: "There won't be any sermon today." There is a case to be made for banning sermons for some time and instead showing an icon, a picture or a caption. I think Chrysologus would give such advice. His gift was giving short, two or three-line sermons. The name means eloquent preacher. Brevity does not mean lack of truth or content. This was his sermon style: "That God is found in flesh is an honour for the creature, not a humiliation for the Creator. So why have you such a low opinion of yourself when you are so precious to God?" Another: "Hasn't the whole universe been made for you? For you the earth is embroidered with flowers."

31 JULY

Ignatius of Loyola – Spain – 16th century

Waiting in an x-ray room there was a display of colour magazines, to interest us in the goings-on of the personalities of the day. There was also a "Thought for the Day" book, drab and worn looking. Ignatius was an enthusiastic reader, interested in the goings-on and excitement of the day. It was only by accident that he picked up a Thought for the Day from a *Life of Christ* and the Saints. Somehow, the excitement he got from the magazines did not match the excitement that stayed with him after reading the *Life of Christ.* So he decided to follow that scent. He became one of the great inspirations of the Christian world. Laugh, he said, and grow strong. It is a real blessing to get an interest in knowing God more. Books become treasure. With the great Second Vatican Council the Spirit has let loose renewed ideas of God. A fresh spirituality, especially in the reading and understanding of the Scriptures.

August

1 AUGUST

Alfonsus Liguori – Italy – 18th century

I did not like much the Redemptorist missions of long ago. But I sure did admire their enthusiasm. Alphonsus was an enthusiastic young lawyer. Because of a setback, he decided to seek fulfilment elsewhere – with God's poor and neglected. His enthusiasm helped him to live to the ripe old age of 91 years, despite an enormous workload and plenty of frustrations. He said that things that we think are misfortunes in life, from God's point of view are blessings. God uses a chisel to carve us into his masterpieces.

2 AUGUST

Eusebius of Vercilli – Italy – 4th century

We are easily led at times. Some commentators say that there are no morals today, and less church-going. One wonders what that has to do with my appreciation of the day's sunshine, fresh air or water. Am I that flabby, soft and lazy in my thinking that if somebody breaks a leg, I give up walking? Eusebius had his own viewpoint. He took on no less a power than the Emperor Constantius. Constantius might be ruler of the east, but he was not God. It suited his authority to deny that Jesus was God, because it kept God authoritarian, rather than intimate with us, his poor and imperfect children. Eusebius was released from captivity, after the death of Constantius in 361 AD.

3 AUGUST

Lydia – Palestine – 1st century

I was once asked to negotiate the setting up of a new parish community. It involved buying land for schools, church and community centre. I went to the landowner with fear and the uncertainty of inexperience. I was welcomed at the door and offered a cup of tea. That was the first link in a chain, that now encircles a community of teeming young life, schools, a community centre and church. Lydia was the first to welcome Paul in Philippi. She was a businesswoman. She not only accepted the Good News of Jesus Christ, but offered Paul the hospitality of bed and board as well. Maybe, without her support, Paul might never have kept going. Whether we are rich or poor we are gifted by God. With daily courtesies of being able to smile, say welcome, have a drink. These are the everyday miracles of life.

4 AUGUST

Oswald – England – 7th century

Oswald's father was King of Northumbria. Oswald fled for his life. He took refuge in the Monastery of Iona. He became Christian, and later returned with his family to Northumbria when the tyrant, Edwin, had died. I'm sure that Oswald would have thought that leaving, to go into exile, was a disaster, failure and loss. Yet, were it not for that happening he might never have heard the Good News of Jesus Christ that he embraced on Iona. He longed to share that Good News with his people in Northumbria. He returned to die a martyr. Jesus Christ failed and yet the failure was full of blessing. Often, when we fail we can learn our own limitations, and we can become less judgemental, more compassionate, and trusting in the God who accepts our humanity totally in all its weakness.

5 AUGUST

John Mary Vianney – France – 19th century

I am sure that John Mary Vianney, Patron of Parish priests, will forgive us for being a day late with his feast. He is also the patron of being able to wait on others with loving attention. His secret, I think, was his intimate chats with God. Like Jesus' teaching that God's spirit is given to every child that is called to be born, the spirit, or angel is appointed to each for the journey of life. John Vianney used to say that talking to our personal spirit or angel was like lighting one straw, but when we join with others, like "praying Mass together" it is like a bundle of straws together making a warm fire of praise to God.

6 AUGUST

Transfiguration of Jesus on Mount Tabor – 1st century

What did he see in her or she in him, the neighbours asked. Love sees beauty, and common goodness as charm, where reason sees only ordinary drabness. Peter, James and John went to the mountain with Jesus. The experience transformed them. They saw humanity in a new light. Thomas Merton, Trappist monk, lived in solitude. One day, in a large city, he had a similar vision. In a busy street he saw thousands of ordinary people. They were shining like stars of unbelievable beauty. He was overawed by the love of the compassionate Father who embraces humanity in its dregs, though tattered and torn. People are God's delight. Such insight of heart and mind transforms the world.

7 AUGUST

Cajetan – Italy – 16th century

Cajetan studied law, but he felt drawn to the poor and the incurable. He became a priest and was one of the world's great reformers. The Good Shepherd, the best reformer, has to be ahead of the sheep, but not so far in front that they cannot recognise him. Cajetan experienced all kinds of opposition in trying to implement his reforming ideals. But his love of the poor and the weak kept him closely in touch with the frailty of our graced humanity. People are more important than ideas. Liturgy celebrates people in God – primary – the rules of the celebration are secondary.

8 AUGUST

Dominic – Spain – 12th century

Dominic brought a fresh understanding of God and put new clothes on him that appealed to ordinary people. Just as the Spirit of God, through the Second Vatican

Council, put fresh ideas of God and inspiring thoughts of humanity and the world, before us for our blessing. The Albigensians were honest in their criticism of the ills and corruptions of the Church, but they were misguided in the severity of their methods. Dominic stepped into the breach. Reform that is not scented with compassion is not of God. Dominic was a happy man, of pleasant countenance. A nun was fascinated by his beautiful eyes. His teaching reflected his personality. His love of God had moved from head to heart. He founded the Order of Preachers, the Dominicans. To give up on God, Church or charity because of the sins of others, is a false trail. It is giving up on oneself. If the problem is sinners then I can head the list. Life is living with failure.

9 AUGUST

Edith Stein – Germany – 20th century

Edith Stein died in the Concentration Camp of Auschwitz in 1942. She had become a Carmelite nun. She wrote from prison and said that while she had chosen a life of seclusion, God does not always promise that seclusion. She loved and celebrated the sacraments of the Church, but God is not tied to sacraments only. God compensates in many other ways, she said. Her's indeed was an expansive idea of God's presence. We are never really alone. The family was worried where Grandad would be buried. He said, "It doesn't matter. God will find me wherever I am."

10 AUGUST

Lawrence – Italy – 3rd century

Lawrence was ordered to give up the Church's treasures to the Emperor Valerian. He was given three days to obey the command. During that time he gathered together the poor, misfits, the down-and-outs in Rome and brought them to the Emperor. "Here are my treasures", he said. He was martyred. Mother Teresa of Calcutta saw deprived and abandoned children as Treasures. She found the secret of her respect in celebrating daily Mass. She touched the hem of his garment in Holy Communion and in the strength of that food and Christ's love, her heart was warmed to embrace God's wounded of this earth.

11 AUGUST

Clare – Italy – 13th century

Clare was born into a family of wealth and plenty. But when she met St Francis, she was so taken by his spirit that she ran away from her castle home to join him. She had her golden hair cut off and wore a sack habit. What a shock for her parents. Later, Francis found a house for her to start the Poor Clares. She was joined by her sister Agnes and her mother. Although Clare never left Assisi her impact on the world was immense. Despite the solitude of her life, she was always with the people of Assisi in their trials and troubles. God writes straight with crooked lines. God is full of surprises. The human heart can always be touched by God's spirit in every circumstance of life and in ways we never dream or imagine. So it is unwise to hold judgements about people. We never really know the full story. There is always more to be seen than meets the eye.

12 AUGUST

Euplius – Italy – 4th century

Euplius was martyred with the *Gospels* around his neck. It was not so much the book, as the message of Jesus Christ's Good News that inspired Euplius. People sometimes say that the dullest part of church is the reading of the Scripture stories. People complain that readings are often unintelligible, unheard and poorly celebrated. I like to think of the Scriptures as God's love letters. I am loved totally and without condition by the compassionate Father who writes these letters for our encouragement. Not to take a love letter with delight – not to want to sift the meaning and words is a loss. To read, not wanting to delight and encourage people, is not good enough. The Church of Vatican II has wonderfully renewed the treasures of sacred Scripture, but some would say that the scent of God's unbelievable love in his word has yet to be smelt.

13 AUGUST

Rose Schlosinger – Germany – 20th century

Rose joined a resistance group in Germany during World War II. She was condemned to death. She wrote to her young daughter from prison. She expressed the wish that her daughter would find the love that she had found with her husband Bodo. Learn to wait for a love that will share all suffering and all difficulties with you, and such may your love be too. When we have to die, we are sorry for every unkind word we have said of loved ones. Every day is precious. It is a pity that even a minute is spent in sadness. The human spirit is greater than any obstacle.

14 AUGUST

Maximilian Kolbe – Poland – 20th century

I remember a huge banner, held by two young people, in St Peter's Square, Rome, at the canonisation of Maximilian Kolbe in 1982. Maximilian was portrayed in splendour in red vestments, with Franciscan sandals. He was enveloped in white clouds, and greeted by an angel of resurrection and gracious Mother Mary. At his feet lay a minuscule, emaciated body, twisted up in death on a prison floor with an injecting needle in the arm. The other memory I have is of the Polish sergeant, Francis Gazowniczek, the one whose life was saved when Maximilian volunteered to take his place in the death chamber. He was present at the canonisation. I wondered what his thoughts were. The seed of glory sown in man, will flower when we see God's face.

15 AUGUST

Mary's Assumption

Little John asked, "Is Grandad dead?" His mother said, "Yes, Grandad is dead and gone to Heaven." "Mother", he said, "is Grandad alive in Heaven?" "Yes, he is." "How come if he was dead, he is alive in Heaven?" "Listen", his mother said, "God gives him a big kiss and that makes him alive in Heaven". John said, "Mother, that must be a fabulous kiss." The feast of Mary Assumed into Heaven celebrates that kiss. We bless rose petals today as we celebrate what God's love has in store for us. Every petal is a little kiss of God and reminds us of Mary, our special rose, and God, the giver of roses.

16 AUGUST

Stephen of Hungary – 11th century

Stephen was the first Christian King of Hungary. He made a rule that every tenth town would build a church for the people. Stephen saw the church as a vital link in the service of God in the lives of people. I often explain to the little ones that we come to church to pray together, to pray for each other's needs. It is God's world, it is God's invitation. If we don't want to pray together, then we are free to walk, to watch TV or play games. It is a sad family when some opt out of being generous to one another. Doing things together, supporting one another, is good family spirit; it is hardly fair to leave all the work to the others. Church-going is a family exercise for God's sake and the neighbours'.

17 AUGUST

Roch – France – 14th century

Roch is always painted with a dog. The dog is carrying bread in his mouth. When Roch, the hermit got ill in the woods his dog brought food to keep him alive. When my favourite dog... 'Kerri' died I wanted to say, "Lord, thank you for all the joy, love and humour that you have given me through this gifted little dog. The enthusiasm of his welcomes, the excitement of his friendship, his soothing cuddles, his gratitude for little favours, his god-like faithfulness, his ways of relaxing, his little tricks of naughtiness. His tail wagged an endless... Thank you... to life even in his final sleeping moments. Such beauty and loveliness cannot be lost. There is pain, but somehow it is pain that one would not have wanted to miss, because of the treasure that lay hidden within it.

18 AUGUST

Helena – Bithynia – 3rd century

Helena's son was Constantine, the first Christian Emperor. He was the first emperor to give freedom to Christianity. He also released all religious prisoners. Helena had been divorced by the Roman emperor, Constantius Chlorus. Helena too became Christian, not only in name, but in deed. Perhaps she should be the patroness of the divorced and separated. People suffer great stress and pain in broken relationships, and often are made to feel worthless and failures. Often we judge ourselves too harshly and even absent ourselves from God's church and table. The compassionate Father welcomes all, and understands failing, and always invites us, not because we are perfect, but because God is good and we are human and frail.

19 AUGUST

John Eudes – France – 17th century

Jesus wanted to change people's idea of God. He was not the judgemental spy in the sky, the spoilsport, wanting to catch us out. God is the compassionate Father, who always welcomes us in rags or riches. John Eudes took this teaching to heart. But he met stiff opposition from the Jansenists who taught about the harshness of God and the restrictions of salvation. When John befriended the prostitutes, his motives were misunderstood. He promoted devotion to the Sacred Heart and the Heart of Mary, and provided the ideas that launched the Good Shepherd Sisters. When he found difficulty with people, which seemed quite often, he prayed to his opponent's guardian angel for help.

20 AUGUST

Bernard – France – 12th century

Bernard is called the second founder of the Cistercians. He arrived with thirty others at the gates of the monastery of Stephen Harding. Stephen was about to give up.

Bernard became, not only Man of the Year, but Man of the Century in Europe. How he combined such an active, busy life with monastic mysticism reminds me of the Gabrielle Bossis story. She was a well-to-do person, a travelling mystic in our century. She was prompted by an inner voice that said, "You tell me all that happens to you, I love to hear. Name people to me." The voice said, "Your imagination is like a house dog that wanders here and there." Don't we like a dog that roams? The voice said, "You will never be perfect. Get used to trying to love." She prayed, "Lord, shine through your little girl." I am sure Bernard would understand.

21 AUGUST

Pius 10th – Italy – 20th century

Pius was one of ten children from a poor Italian family. He felt awkward with the trappings of authority. As Pope he had to wear prescribed clothes. He complained: "Look how they have dressed me up, and I am led around by soldiers like Jesus in Gethsemane." Putting on the uniform is important in the kitchen, on the job. It really means taking responsibility for others. Pius did just that. But taking off the uniform is important too. We are forever human, frail instruments of God's goodness. Sometimes the uniform can give that haughty look that never saw beauty in book or brook.

22 AUGUST

Antoine Frederic Ozanam – France – 19th century

We don't give up going to the doctor because somebody dies. We don't stop eating because somebody gets ill. We don't retire from football because a player makes a foul. Antoine Frederick Ozanam did not opt out of God, people and religion when France was anti-God, anti-religion and anti-Church, after the Revolution. He believed in God as the compassionate Father and saw his life as caring for the poor and the deprived. Although a young man, and an intellectual, he founded the Vincent de Paul Society in 1833, which has now spread its caring branches all around the world. I recall some of his sayings: "Poverty is any kind of deprivation." "Some people hope, some doubt, some curse, others believe and wait. I am among those who believe and wait for God and for country."

23 AUGUST

Philip Benizi – Italy – 13th century

Philip was a brilliant scholar. He tried to hide his light by becoming a gardener. He was caught out and given weighty responsibility in the Servite Order. He hid again in the woods when there was talk of him being elected Pope. Philip had the idea that true responsibility can only be exercised if one is held by the hand of God. It is easy to forget the all-giving hand.

24 AUGUST

Bartholemew – Palestine – 1st century

Michelangelo felt that he got a raw deal from some of the ecclesiastical authorities. In one of his masterpieces he represents himself as a Bartholemew, being flayed to death. Bartholemew had the experience of being with Jesus and meeting the Lord on the seashore after his resurrection. His vision of God and life made him do great things for others, but there is no love without sacrifices.

25 AUGUST

Joseph Calasanz – Spain – 17th century

His ambition was to take the children off the streets of Rome and to provide schools for their education. He met with hot opposition, because people knew that when the poor were educated, they would make demands. He was also harassed for sending children to the great scientist Galileo, who was then under a cloud of suspicion. His community was suppressed. Only after his death were they restored to religious status. Parents and people never see the full fruit of their actions, nor does the blossom ever see the seed. A seed of goodness and kindness can take years to mature in a person's heart, and bring about change. It all makes life hereafter, the full harvesting, an interesting prospect.

26 AUGUST

Zephyrinus – Italy – 3rd century

A visit to the catacombs of St Callistus is an abiding memory of Rome. It is getting in touch with the roots of the Christian message. There are hundreds of underground tombs, where the martyred Christians were buried during persecution. This burial place was acquired by Zephyrinus, the fifteenth Pope of Rome. The catacombs became hiding places to celebrate Christian liturgies. One of the earliest images of Christ that is etched on the wall of a catacomb shows Jesus as Good Shepherd. For the early Christians the Good News was simply – God is Good Shepherd, compassionate, protective and Saviour.

27 AUGUST

Monica – North Africa – 4th century

A blessing from parents gives roots of security and wings of encouragement. Monica did not clip the wings of her wayward son, Augustine, but she certainly kept a flexible hold on him. She pursued him relentlessly with her prayers. The challenge of parents to love the child is the greatest in all the world. It is interesting that when Augustine had turned around, and if you like, achieved sainthood, his mother Monica died. Maybe her mission was accomplished, but also she had achieved her life's ambition. It is strange, that often we are at our best when we are in the thick of the fray, struggling to rear children, pay bills, cope with sickness, get on in life. Many grandparents tell me that those were the best days. We felt needed. Monica's only request to Augustine was to remember her at the altar of the Lord.

28 AUGUST

Augustine – Algeria – 4th century

Augustine was one of the world's most enthusiastic lovers. His influence on the Christian scene has been immense over the centuries. He prayed: "Lord, make me pure, but not yet." He struggled to give his heart to God, realising: "Lord, you have made us for yourself, and our hearts are restless until they rest in you". Kill the error, he said, but love the erring. I recall the gist of his writings in the Confessions: "Too late have I loved you, O beauty, ever ancient, ever new. You were with me, but I was not with you. Things held me from you, things which if they were not in you, were not at all. You called and burst my deafness. You flashed and shone and scattered my blindness. Your breathed odours and I drew in breath, you touched me and I burned for your peace."

29 AUGUST

John the Baptist – Palestine – 1st century

John lost his head for humanity. Jesus lost his heart through humanity. John's image of God was judgemental – prepare fire for the great retribution. Jesus' image of God was the compassionate Father, who loves even the weakest and greatest sinner. In prison John asked: "Are you the one who is to come?" We battle with the same images today. Which image is my God? Which image does Jesus teach in his unforgettable stories, The Lost Son, The Lost Sheep, The Lost Coin, The Good Samaritan?

30 AUGUST

Fiacra, – Ireland – 7th century

France won the Rose of Tralee Beauty Contest in 1997. Their representative was a young Irish girl working in France. A young Irishman named Fiacra also won honours for France and his name has been remembered for over a thousand years. He set up a hermitage there and sought out the deprived, built a hospice for the poor, and helped the farmers. There is a St Fiacra Hotel in Paris. The first four-wheeled cab was called The Fiacra, because it taxied people to St Fiacra's shrine. The good that people do lives on.

31 AUGUST

Joseph Muller – Germany – 20th century

In August 1944 a German priest was in prison awaiting execution for his stand against the Hitler regime. He wrote his last letter from his cell, saying that his heart was full of joy, awaiting his new birthday with God. He thanked the world, his faithful cell – a silent friend, his last church and pulpit. He thanked the people he had served in streets and lanes and places, the kind people and the not so kind. Goodbye to my home, my place of work, and blessed be Jesus Christ.

September

1 SEPTEMBER

Giles – Greece – 7th century

While Giles was sheltering a hunted deer in his hut, he himself was shot by an arrow. It was a blessing in disguise. The king built a monastery for him, and his kindly influence spread far and wide. With his respect for the animal kingdom, Giles believed that the message of Christ was a plan for all the world, not just human souls. That plan of God is now present. His Kingdom is in our world.

2 SEPTEMBER

Diana, Princess of Wales – England
– 20th century

The world mourned the Princess of Wales. She had a tragic accident in Paris. Her loveliness seems to have moved all hearts, young and old, male and female, secular and religious. She touched with hand and heart the untouchables of the world on her missions of caring. She drew the world's attention to the awfulness of hidden landmines that destroyed innocent human life every day. Her own weaknesses and vulnerability made her humanly attractive. Her favourite lines, in a poem, said – "Remember me and the love we shared, and always know we cared." Her candle may have gone out, but her legend lives on.

3 SEPTEMBER

Gregory the Great – Italy – 6th century

Gregory was the first monk to become Pope. His achievements have influenced the world for over a thousand years, not least with Gregorian Chant. And sending St Augustine as a missionary to England. His ideas are very encouraging. He said, "When I was a monk I could keep my tongue from idle topics, but now my mind is distracted with many responsibilities as an everyday person. Because I am weak myself I am drawn into idle talk and I find myself saying the kind of things that I did not even care to listen to before." "What kind of watchman am I?" he asked. "I don't stand on the pinnacle of achievement. I languish rather in the depths of weakness and yet my Redeemer, though I am unworthy, gives me the grace to see life whole and the power to speak effectively of it. Perhaps my very recognition of failure will win me pardon from the sympathetic judge."

4 SEPTEMBER

Rose of Viterbo – Italy – 13th century

Rose was an only child. Yet her impact for good was so extraordinary that the Emperor Frederick banished her and her family from Viterbo. But Rose continued her crusade in other towns and villages. Weakness is no shame in God's loving plan. Through our very weakness God's blessings become obvious. The whole world was touched by the young Princess Diana's death. Through her pain and vulnerability and motherly care, her humanity was beautified, and people liked that scent.

5 SEPTEMBER

Lawrence Justinian – Italy – 15th century

Lawrence was known as a great gift-giver. God's gifts come wrapped for us in all kinds of varieties. We receive life, but we grow more human by being gift-givers. Perhaps we think of gifts too much in terms of money. We have a good capacity for joy and also the ability to give joy in so many ways. Remembering the birthday, the anniversary, the success news, complimenting people on their retirement – a bright smile saying thanks.

6 SEPTEMBER

Mother Teresa – Albania – 20th century

She gave her life to bring love to the dying and destitute, especially abandoned children on the streets and in the slums of Calcutta. She was once asked why she did not enlarge her mission and her thoughts to the millions of other starving children. She said: "God asked me to be faithful, not successful." God does not ask us to control everything, but to be faithful to the daily routine of children, work, friends and neighbours. To trust in the middle of darkness, temptation and worries. This is faithfulness to the good God.

7 SEPTEMBER

Peter Claver – Spain – 17th century

When the negro slave trade from Africa to Central America was rampant Peter Claver met the slave ships at a port of call in Columbia, Cartegena. He would attend the dying, bring food and drink to half-crazed prisoners. He brought the message of Christ, through interpreters. Perhaps it is drug slavery that is the curse of our day. It promises happiness, but brings disaster and death. Our mission is to educate our children, know the language and the terms of the drug world. Our mission, too, is to help victims and their families to make a stand and to pray for drug-pushers.

8 SEPTEMBER

The Birth of Mary – Palestine – 1st century

Mary was born in the mind of God, through her native people, and in the womb of her mother Anna. We too have such births. God, country, mother and father. One imagines that Mary was a very loved child. Her coming was welcomed and looked forward to by her parents. Anna would have told Mary of God the compassionate Father whose love for the human is unbelievable and unconditional. Some children never experience that kind of love, nor that image of God. Surely, Mary will have a great welcome for the unloved of this world.

9 SEPTEMBER

Ciaran – Ireland – 6th century

Ciaran died at Clonmacnoise at 33 years of age. Silent stones mark his resting place. He chose the most beautiful place for his monastery, because God, for him, was beauty. The lovely Shannon river turns to pay respect to his memory. The sky is endless, the meadow lands mystical. His monastery flourished for a thousand years. Scholars came from all over Europe to study here and some of the High Kings of Ireland are buried here. Its vacancy is full of sound. The Cross of the Scriptures stands with awesome beauty to the memory of King Flann. On it Ciaran is chiselled in stone, staking his monastery, hand in hand with rebel King Dermot, who gave him this land. Ciaran is God's peacemaker.

10 SEPTEMBER

Nicholas of Tolentino – Italy – 13th century

Nicholas was an eloquent preacher. He touched the hearts of thousands. I wonder about the secret and success of his preaching. Some theologians say that preaching today is too much preoccupied with moral teaching, with the idea of doing things to earn Heaven. They argue that this is a false principle. Christianity is not about laws and sin primarily. It is based on the compassionate Father and the unconditional love of God. When we trust the Father, then activities happen, towards others and towards real life. People long for the God of compassion and kindness and what touches everyday reality in their lives. Better to remind people of their dignity as human beings, before asking them to respond. After all the Angel complimented Mary first.

11 SEPTEMBER

Etty Hillesum – Amsterdam – 20th century

Etty Hillesum was a single girl. In response to a voice in her heart she volunteered to go with her Jewish people on the death train to Auschwitz in September 1943. She died there. She has been called the mystic who lived in Hell. She was a deeply human person. It was love that coloured all her relationships in life, and indeed, imperfect relationships at times, that are not without humour. A note from her on the death train said, "This is the happiest moment. I pray, O God, take me with your great hands and turn me into your instrument, to be humbly available to my people. To uplift them with a word, just to be there. With the passing of people I feel a growing need to speak to you alone. In every human being I love something of you, my God."

12 SEPTEMBER

Guy – Belgium – 11th century

Guy took on the work of sacristan in the church at Laeken, Brussels. Although very devoted to the care of the church, he was even more devoted to the care of the poor. A businessman impressed by his generosity asked him to be a partner in a merchant business. I'm sure he thought this was a message from Heaven. He left his job reluctantly. Shortly afterwards the merchant's ship sank and the business collapsed. Also his church job had been given away to another. Although losing all, he did not get embittered, but rather accepted his fate. The Lord giveth, the Lord taketh away. Blessed be the name of the Lord. We don't have to be successful to be accepted by God. We are always his precious sons and daughters.

13 SEPTEMBER

John Chrysostom – Syria – 5th century

The name means "Golden Mouthed". He was a very gifted speaker and exponent of the Gospel truth. The ordinary people applauded him in church because of his ideas of sharing wealth with the poor. He incurred the wrath of Queen Eudoxia, who sent him into exile. Seekers of truth and real justice are often disliked and threatened. It is one thing to comfort the disturbed, but mostly the comfortable don't like to be disturbed. Maybe the resentment and opposition we sometimes have against the new idea, the new book, the new arrival in work or in the neighbourhood, is because our comfortable stance is challenged.

14 SEPTEMBER

The Triumph of the Cross

Early Irish art dressed Jesus in kingly robes, nailed to the cross. He looks serene, with open eyes, loving the world. The artists saw the crucifixion of Jesus as victory. He is alive and with us now. Many things happen in life by chance, rather than by choice. Crosses come our way in all shapes and sizes, uninvited. Indeed, sometimes we make our own crosses. Jesus, who walks the journey of life before us, asks us not to be afraid, to trust. Nothing happens without God's providence. St Thérèse of Lisieux said: "If God allows me the cross, God also gives me the strength to bear and cope."

15 SEPTEMBER

Mary of Sorrows – Palestine – 1st century

Her young son died mysteriously. Her eldest daughter was murdered four weeks later and her younger daughter was brutally beaten in the defence of four little children. I was privileged to sit with the mother and father during that human tragedy. I was greatly helped by the image of Mary standing by the cross during the horror of her Son's crucifixion. I had no words to say, nor did it seem necessary. Mary said no words. She stood there. It was enough to be just standing there, being present in support. I listened to understandable words of anger, but also words of loveliness about the goodness of life, despite all.

16 SEPTEMBER

Cornelius – Italy – 3rd century

Why don't people go to church nowadays, I am often asked. Pope Paul VI said that non-practising is not new in the history of the world, but is the result of natural weakness and a profound inconsistency deep in our make-up. He said that it is the gentle action of the Spirit that brings interior change. So respect peoples religious situation. "People are spiritual in ways we do not see." Concern for this earth, concern for the poor. Pope John Paul II asked us to respect people in the different stages of the journey of life. Cornelius was one of the first Popes to take a compassionate stand against rigorism, to let those who had fallen away from the Church, through persecution, be welcomed back into the fold. He had bitter opposition from the anti-Pope Novatian. We can put no limit on God's love, is the constant teaching of the Church.

17 SEPTEMBER

Robert Bellarmine – Italy – 16th century

Nobody has monopoly of truth. Although Bellarmine was one of the great minds of the world, he was mistaken in his thinking about the scientist Galileo. He was not mistaken in his concern for the poor. He gave away the curtains in his drawing room to those who were shivering and without clothes. He said, "The walls won't catch cold." It is easy to get cluttered up with all kinds of things in life, yet there are no pockets in a shroud. It is wise to try to "hang loose", not to be possessed by any person or thing. Really, nobody owns anybody.

18 SEPTEMBER

Joseph of Cupertino – Italy – 17th century

Joseph was an extraordinary man. He was born in a shed, rejected by his mother, called the "gaper" because he went around with his mouth open. He lost his job because he was breaking the plates and dishes and forgot to light the fire. When he became a priest, it is said, he could take flight during Mass. He became an embarrassment to his fellow priests and he had to be hidden away from the people in their curiosity. He was forbidden to say Mass. People in love do extraordinary things. If we are loved, or feel we are in love, and being appreciated, we feel like jumping over the moon. We can be so magnanimous and in love with the world, everybody we meet, everything we see. Joseph caught the love of God in its depth. The results were extraordinary. Psalm 110 says: "Lord, make me remember your wonders. The Lord is compassion and love." Joseph lived by these words.

19 SEPTEMBER

Theodore – Greece – 7th century

Some people have a thing about age. We forget the poets who tell us that youthfulness is in one's spirit. It is not in wrinkles or grey hairs. The spirit that wants to enthuse, to appreciate, to find joy in helping another, is perpetually young. Rembrand, the artist, catches this truth in the faces of the aged. Perhaps it is when we neglect the spirit, the mystical, the mystery, that old age preoccupies. Theodore came from Rome to Canterbury, with the Good News of Jesus Christ in the year 667. He was then 65 years of age. He made a greater impact in England than even Augustine. He set up schools in Canterbury that attracted scholars from all over Europe. He was one of the great peacemakers of his time, a bridge-builder between many peoples.

20 SEPTEMBER

Thomas Johnston and companions – England – 16th century

Although they were hermits in solitude, they seemed a threat to Henry VIII. He had some starved to death and others executed at Tyburn. Those great people spotlight for us the extraordinary blessing of freedom and choice, of saying yes or no. It is an awesome gift. We can be deprived of everything, but not of conscience. Sometimes we get over-stressed in life because of our inability to say no. We would like to say yes to what's important, and no to what's urgent.

21 SEPTEMBER

Matthew – Palestine – 1st century

Tax collectors are not over-popular, even today, but they are very necessary. If the tax collector works for an occupying army, he is despised. Yet Matthew, the tax collector, was the one Jesus chose to broadcast the Good News of the compassionate Father. Matthew weaves the message of God's unbelievable and unconditional love into his genealogy of Jesus. This story of Jesus' family contains as many sinners as saints. Outsiders in every sense, including five women. Matthew has grasped the insight of a God whose unconditional love is not dependent of human merit. A God who does not hesitate to use the scheming as well as the noble, the impure as well as the pure. This God continues to work through us today.

22 SEPTEMBER

Thomas of Villanueva – Spain – 16th century

My very good friend was going through a bad patch in his marriage. He took a temporary separation to think things over. His little girl of ten went to town with her mother one day to buy shoes. In the excitement she walked across a busy street and was struck by a passing motor car. She was thrown into the air and landed on her bottom on the footpath. There was consternation but miraculously no bone was broken, just bruises and scratches. As her mother wept in shock, the little girl said: "Mam, come and buy me the shoes." The mother contacted her husband that night. He was devastated. He returned home immediately to a great reunion. Their marriage began anew again. With that incident a whole new perspective of life opened. He said that he was exaggerating trivialities. How short life can be and how precious is his little child. It was by accident, too, a mistake, that Thomas of Villanueva became Archbishop and a saint.

23 SEPTEMBER

Constantius – Italy

A little child was asked if she saw Holy God in her visit to the church. She said: "I didn't, but I saw his Mammy working in the back of the church." There should be a saint for sacristans, for people who work in the back of the church and in front of the church and all around the church. Life would be impossible in church without the never-ending planning and watchful eye of the sacristan. It is a great peace, celebrating Mass, to know somebody is there in case of emergency: a child lighting candles, someone else having a fight. Constantius was sacristan in the Cathedral of Ancona. He was on a ladder one day, attending candles, when a disturbed man wandered into the church looking for the sacristan. He abused verbally the man on the ladder. The saintly man got down off the ladder, shook his hand and said: "I'm glad somebody sees through me."

24 SEPTEMBER

Our Lady of Mercy – Spain – 13th century

Every era and culture has its particular qualities and laws. Paying ransom to liberate people was a way of life for many hundreds of years. Peter Nolasco founded a society to ransom Christian slaves from the Saracens. He pledged his work to Mary, Our Lady of Mercy. Whatever the human condition, whatever the age, time or place, Mary has a motherly care for her wounded sons and daughters. People reflect this encouraging belief in the many devotions and prayers to Mary, who always prays for us now, and at the hour of death.

25 SEPTEMBER

Finbar "Barry" – Ireland – 7th century

Finbar means the "fair-headed one". It is a name revered in County Cork, Ireland. Finbar must have had a sunshine idea of God too. He choose Gougane Barra as a place of solitude. It is an idyllic island. The gentle water lapping the shore soothes the ear. The beauty of mountain, trees and passing clouds, delight the eye. On my last visit there a wedding was being celebrated in the small church beside the lakeshore. I think Finbar saw God's world and God's people as a fantastic wedding celebration.

26 SEPTEMBER

Cosmas and Damian – Syria – 4th century

It is said that the good we do lives after us. Cosmos and Damian were healers who gave their services free because of their Christian faith. They were martyred. Their names remain. Yet little is known of their history. In Christian teaching, God's plan is for the whole world, people and nature. How all that happens will harmonise under God's providence is an exciting concept. Jesus encourages the getting together process. The true Christian is a bridge-builder, a peacemaker, a harmoniser, a lover of earth.

27 SEPTEMBER

Vincent de Paul – France – 17th century

Our God image is often shaped by the image of our parents. If we have had bad childhood experiences, it is difficult to see God as loving Father/Mother, so many people say that a healing image of God is our greatest need and best prayer. Vincent de Paul had a grumpy temperament, but he did not let that influence his idea of God as the loving compassionate Father who loves his sons and daughters. We must try to be involved in the cares and sorrows of our brothers and sisters, he said, and pray for the spirit of compassion. Love takes precedence over all. A neighbour's need comes first.

28 SEPTEMBER

Eustochium – Italy – 4th century

Many thoughtful people say that the insights that the Spirit of God gave us in the Second Vatican Council haven't begun to mushroom yet. The treasures are there, but not really opened or aired. One such treasure is the Word of God in the Sacred Scriptures, called by the Council "The Table of the Word". Table suggests vital, life-giving food, warmth, friendship, encouragement, hospitality. The Scriptures are still a closed book for the ordinary person. We need new envelopes for God's Good News. The Great St Jerome said that to be ignorant of the Scriptures is to be ignorant of Christ – of God's wisdom. Jerome was ably assisted by Eustochium in translating the Scriptures fifteen hundred years ago. She was a believer in God's presence in his word.

29 SEPTEMBER

Archangels Michael, Gabriel, Raphael

Michael means "like God". Gabriel means "power of God". Raphael means "healing of God". Celtic spirituality tells that when a person is born a candle is lit in Heaven and the light of that candle shelters the person all through life. There is a kindly presence with us, some call it our guardian angel, others soul, others the divine. Every child should be encouraged to believe in this kindly presence – a soul friend. There comes a realisation then, that one is never alone. The air is full of invisible presence.

When we expect a guideline, a light, it will always be there.

30 SEPTEMBER

Jerome, Dalmatia – Yugoslavia – 4th century

Her marriage failed. She said to her mother: “Mam, I did hear your words of advice not to marry, but I did not ‘feel’ them at that time. I have to feel the words myself.” Faith in the Sacred Scriptures, the Word of God, includes study, but depends on this mysterious feeling in the heart, the love which is a gift of God. When we love in the heart, expression follows. The prayer of the Church gives thanks for Jerome for his deep reverence for the Holy Scriptures, which he loved with all his heart.

October

1 OCTOBER

Thérèse of Lisieux – France – 19th century

Thérèse's message is for today's people. She died at 24 years. She said, poor humans are like frightened rabbits, hounded to death with guilt and failures, but God our Father takes us home as his favourite pets. God, she said, has a fatal flaw in our regard: it is his mercy. I am a little child, too weak to climb the stairs of life, will you, Lord, by my lift? She fell asleep during prayer time, didn't like retreats or community prayers. Her love was the Gospel story. She took the word of Jesus to heart, that God hugs humanity like a little child that is weak. A parent loves a child whether asleep or awake, and so God loves us. If there be a hell, she said, there's nobody in it. I was so low in darkness, suffering and depression, she said, that I would have committed suicide only for trust in God who is love. When she could not receive Communion, she said, so be it, God has other ways of blessing all his people. Hers is a vision of God and life that the world longs for.

2 OCTOBER

Thomas of Hereford – England – 13th century

Thomas was a zealous reforming bishop. He clashed with the Archbishop of Canterbury – John Peckham. John excommunicated Thomas. Thomas went to the Pope to state his case, but died at Orvieto on his return journey, worn out with the struggles of life. His goodness prevailed among the people of Hereford. They acclaimed him. Rejection is not always a bad sign. Only God knows the human heart. His creatures are terribly narrow in their thoughts, so St Thérèse of Lisieux said. Sometimes we impose crosses on ourselves that are not of God's making. We take rigid positions on non-essential issues in the name of conscience, rather than accepting the enlightenment of others and opening the mind.

3 OCTOBER

The Ewalds – England – 7th century

There were two Ewalds, one the dark, the other the fair. They were born in Northumbria and educated in Ireland. They were murdered in Germany as missionaries because of fear of Christianity. It is not easy to see how a message of love, for God and one another, could be a threat or bring fear. We feel insecure and threatened by change, especially the change of new ideas. Perhaps that is why the Good Lord constantly tells us not to be afraid, to be open to the risk of loving.

4 OCTOBER

Francis of Assisi – Italy – 13th century

Francis of Assisi is everybody's friend. He saw the face of God in the beauty of the sun, in sister earth, in lady poverty, in the leper, the outcast and the poor. The spirit of Francis lives in the song: "Make me a channel of your peace, where there is hatred let me bring your love, where there is injury, your pardon, Lord, and where there's doubt, true faith in you. O Master, grant that I may never seek so much to be consoled as to console, to be understood as to understand, to be loved, as to love with all my soul."

5 OCTOBER

Raymond of Capua – Italy – 14th century

Catherine of Siena is acclaimed as one of the great Christian women of the world, yet many of her thoughts and ideas would not have come to us were it not for Raymond of Capua, who was her priest friend, and recorded her messages. God uses the weak things of the world to enlighten us. Everything that exists has a voice. Looking at a flower with attention, opens to us worlds of beauty, mystery and exquisite artistry.

6 OCTOBER

Bruno – Germany – 11th century

Bruno was a man for all seasons. Although successful in the everyday world of organising things, he hankered after a life of solitude. It was Bishop St Hugh of Grenoble who gave him and six companions approval, and a piece of land in Chartreuse; so began the great Carthusian Order of monks. The Pope called him to Rome to advise on Church reform. He was a reluctant traveller and eventually escaped back to his monastery. It is true to say that there can be many vocations in one lifetime. St Thérèse of Lisieux exemplifies this truth. She says, love is a vocation that includes all others. She was a powerful missionary, yet never left her convent to go to the missions. It is the little things, done with love, that are blessings. The everyday person in the home, at work, in whatever situation, can be the messenger of love.

7 OCTOBER

Mary of the Rosary – Palestine – 1st century

We are encouraged by many Popes to pray the Rosary. The Rosary is called the ordinary person's Gospel or Bible. During days when Mass was outlawed, and education was for the few, the Rosary was the people's lifeline to God. They could celebrate joy and new life, trusting in God, and have hope in the depths of darkness and crucifixion. The fifteen mysteries are love events or stories from the life of Christ and Mary. Often when we don't know how to pray, or what to say, it is consoling to pass all our concerns to Mary, who prays for us, now and at the hour of our death.

8 OCTOBER

Thais – Egypt – 4th century

In Amsterdam a little boy asked his father what the beautiful girls in the windows were doing. His father answered: "They give hugs to lonely people." Thais gave lonely people hugs, but decided that it was not the way of life for her. She gave her heart to God in new ways.

The heart is a lonely hunter. The good heart transforms the world. Jesus encourages us to look towards the face of the compassionate Father, rather than turning away from the blessings of life. God loves the world and continues his loving presence among us.

9 OCTOBER

John Leonardi – Italy – 16th century

John Leonardi saw new wonders in the people around him and the world he lived in: Pope and prisoner, lay person and saint, young people and old. He minded Philip Neri's cat while he was in Rome. He founded the Order of the Mother of God. He was inspired by the reforms of the Council of Trent. He said to the Pope: "One must look first to God, who is good, before moralising." The Second Vatican Council picks up his message for today and unearths new wonders, reminding us that the Kingdom of God is larger than the Church and is present in the world today, breaking in on us. The Kingdom is God's plan for all the world and the Church is a sign or pointer. Jesus asks us not to turn away from the world, but to turn towards the Good News which is the Compassionate Father.

10 OCTOBER

Francis Borgia – Spain – 16th century

The Borgia Popes in Rome lived a high life, but Francis Borgia in Spain lived a full life. Both searched for happiness in this world. But the ways they chose were different: one chose power and conquest, the other love and service. The wife of an international footballer said that her husband did not need to be "tanked up" with drink to express his personality and gifts, but that it was her love that helped him to see that light. Drink, and the many blessings of life, are gifts to be used in moderation for our good and the good of the world at large.

11 OCTOBER

Canice – Ireland – 6th century

A spiritual writer talked about a weeping statue of Mary near his home-town in the country. It has come and gone. Some people were helped, no doubt, but he asked why do we forget the beautiful hillside and landscape that shelters the statue. The luscious green colours, the racing river, the mysterious rock boulders. These have soothed and nourished the human spirit for thousands of years. While a statue is of human making, hills, landscape, the fields, the clouds, are the work of the divine Designer. There is a spirituality deeper than devotions. I think Canice would have liked these ideas. Canice chose the most beautiful places in Ireland and Scotland for his monastic settings. It is said that he could talk to the birds and the mice. He obviously saw all creation as one – God's harmony.

12 OCTOBER

Wilfrid – England – 7th century

Wilfrid was a man who always had to climb the stairs of life, rather than getting the lift. People who try to be honest and conscientious generally meet stairs of opposition. Wilfrid clashed with civil and religious authorities for justice's sake, and justice for him was right relationship with himself, God and others. Getting into trouble is not always a bad sign. The martyr Dietrich Bonhoffer gave his life for justice, saying that he was only a spoke against a wheel of evil. Even though the wheel might seem to win, there is light hidden in the darkness.

13 OCTOBER

Congan – Ireland – 8th century

Congan had to leave Ireland, even though he loved Ireland. The songs of Ireland tell of leaving and loving. The early Irish monks loved God and country. That recipe always means leaving. All of life is a leaving from one stage of development to another. Without change and leaving there is no life. True love calls for leaving behind bitterness, jealousies, prejudices, ingrained ideas that disrespect people of different cultures and places.

The Good Lord was always leaving, may his Spirit guide our ways.

14 OCTOBER

Callistus – Italy – 3rd century

Callistus surely experienced the lows and highs of life. A slave of a Christian master, he mismanaged money and "did time" for his misdemeanour. Later, a woman in high places obtained his release from the Sardinian mines and he got a job from Pope Zephyrinus, minding a Christian cemetery in Rome. When the Pope died the people and priests elected Callistus as Pope. This enraged Hippolytus, who regarded Callistus as unworthy of the high office. Callistus welcomed back to communion people who had done serious crimes and now repented. He accepted and blessed marriages between free women and slaves. He authorised the ordination of a man who had been married three times. He held that mortal sin was not a sufficient reason to depose a bishop. He was martyred during a disturbance at Trastevere in Rome. The Son of Man came eating and drinking. They said, he is a glutton, a drunkard, a lover of tax collectors and those outside the law (Mt 11:19).

15 OCTOBER

Teresa of Avila – Spain – 16th century

Avila is a wonderland, circled by a rosary of ninety castle towers. A silver river embroiders its loveliness.

Here Teresa danced, sang, played music, liked perfume and became God's great lover. Before entering religious life, when a man admired her neat feet, she said take a good look, you won't have a chance again. Avila makes one dream. Those mighty rock boulders of Roman days, what stories they could tell – and those strong ramparts have secret messages. In the midst of this awesome grandeur, I noticed a frail little girl with her dog, searching through the refuse for some food. In a wonderful world too, Teresa saw wounds that needed healing and love, and she did not pass by. From silly devotions and sour-faced saints, she prayed, deliver us, O Lord. Better no convents than melancholic people, she said. The holier you are, the more sociable you should be. She hated business and money dealings, but took it on for love's sake. In her latter years she liked to compliment people, rather than find fault. She wondered whether this was virtue or laziness.

16 OCTOBER

Margaret Mary Alacoque – France – 17th century

The Messenger of the Sacred Heart is a little magazine I like. It always touches on human realities in life today and God's presence in the ordinary. There are helpful hints on how to deal with children and adolescence in family life. I love the art pictures and the commentary which light up the heart and human spirit. It was Margaret Mary Alacoque who reminded us that God's love is big-hearted, always compassionate, always taking delight in his wayward sons and daughters. This was really sunshine from Heaven during days when God was thought of as harsh, moralistic and judgemental.

17 OCTOBER

Ignatius of Antioch – Syria – 1st century

The poet sees the making of bread as a miraculous transformation. There is earth, and sun, and water, and the touch of human hand. Ignatius of Antioch saw himself as bread, coming from God and being transformed into God, through faith in Jesus Christ. On his last journey, to his martyrdom of being eaten by lions, he wrote seven letters of encouragement to others. Death stalks the human condition in many different ways – illness, inadequacy, accident, fear, leave-taking. But for Ignatius death was a friend to lead one through the gate of Paradise and eternal life. Because God is love, there is life in death and life after death. His hand holds us.

18 OCTOBER

Luke – Palestine – 1st century

Luke not only gives us the Christian story, but also gives us the meaning of Christ's life. His three masterpieces are parables about God's mercy. In the parable of the Lost Son there is no reprimand from the Father, no confession to make; the compassionate Father welcomes home unconditionally both sons. Only a foolish shepherd would risk leaving 99 sheep for the one stray, but in the parable of the Lost Sheep God's love is foolishly extravagant in our regard. In the parable of the Lost Coin the finder spent more money on the party afterwards than the coin was worth. God's love focuses on joy and is not penny-pinching. It is said that Luke was close to Mary. He certainly was a feminist in the best sense. He put special emphasis on the female companions with Jesus. He is not afraid to shock us with the wonder of the Good News of Jesus Christ which is full of humanity and mercy.

19 OCTOBER

Isaac Joque – France – 17th century

How much are we expected to do to make a better world, and how much must we leave to God's providence trustingly? St Augustine said, you do as if all depended on self and pray as if all depended on God. It is not an easy balance to find with peace of mind. Mother Teresa said that it was in praying at the Eucharist that she got in touch with the poor. Isaac Joque was the first European to go a thousand miles into Canada to the edge of Lake Superior to preach the Good News of Jesus Christ. He was imprisoned, tortured and rescued. But he felt compelled to go back to his people and to his death. In a letter to his friend he said, "My confidence is in God, who does not need our help for accomplishing his designs. But we must not spoil his work with our shortcomings." I like the image of the father holding the child's hand at a busy pedestrian crossing, while the child's other hand is carefree and doing its own thing.

20 OCTOBER

Paul of the Cross – Italy – 18th century

I met a Passionist priest. He was a gentle person in every sense, but he was deeply anxious and concerned about how to help people in their needs today, how to bring God into their lives. What could he do? Paul of the Cross founded the Passionist Order of priests. He had a great devotion to the Passion of Christ. His preaching attracted people at parish level. Somehow the passionate love of God in his heart made him humanly attractive and inspired him to know what to do. It is a new and different world today. The religious observances of yesterday don't seem to satisfy the spiritual hunger of many of today's people. My friend concluded that we discover God as we journey along today, on the road of life. We have to wait and watch. Take risks, try new ways, respect the spirituality of people, that perhaps we have been blind to because of our own training. We live in an evolving world and cosmos, and God is present. We agreed to avoid tagging people as irreligious because they didn't fit into our mind-set on religion.

21 OCTOBER

Bertilla – Italy – 20th century

She was inspired by Thérèse of Lisieux who said: "Love makes all vocations." Bertilla was judged not worthy for religious life, but somehow she got in by the back door, working in the bake house and laundry. She graduated as a nurse and became outstanding through her loving care of the sick. It is the love we bring to the job of life that makes all the difference in everyday events. Feeling and passion are beautiful gifts of God. Religion, like love, is more heart than head. When we really love and care we find all kinds of ways of making people feel good and of being compassionate.

22 OCTOBER

Timothy Giaccardo – Italy – 20th century

I am grateful to St Paul's Society for the enthusiasm with which they bring the Good News of God's love to people throughout the world, through writing, art, music, television and radio. Father Alberione was the first person to start a Catholic Press. He gathered around him a few like-minded people who were interested in the mass media. The young Giaccardo was torn between two loves being a priest or dedicating himself to the press. Albertione must have been pleased that he chose the media as his vocation; but later the bishop had a change of heart and let Giaccardo become a priest. So Giaccardo became the first priest in the Society of St Paul, whose blessings touch us all every moment of the day. It is easy to say that there is no life without change, but new wine is not always a popular taste. We are asked to face risks for God's Kingdom, to find new ways to praise the Father that are in tune with the hearts of people and everyday events.

23 OCTOBER

John Capistrano – Italy – 15th century

It is easy to forget the good work that prison tries to do. The prison aims at reform, to heal the person, rather than to punish. John Capistrano reformed when he went to prison. He became an inspiration for Europe. He was chosen by popes for all kinds of charity and peace-making missions. At 70 years of age he led an army against the Turks, in the name of the cross – not a very Christian ideal. But at least he was enthusiastic, if not perfect. Perhaps we need a kind of prison solitude, a desert seclusion, to find our soul, our inner mirror. Like the tree, our human roots go deep down into darkness that is full of life, and we grow outwards to the world with outstretched, branched arms. Without respect for the roots, the branches won't balance. Our inner thoughts, memory, imagination, need time and attention.

24 OCTOBER

Anthony Claret – Spain – 19th century

Anthony knew the art of weaving. There were many threads interwoven in his life. But the overall design was his love of God, expressed in many different locations and vocations. He was missionary, scholar, writer, prisoner, reformer, environmentalist, immigrant, Archbishop and chaplain to Queen Isabella II. "Everybody is asking me for favours", the Queen said to him, "except you." What favour can I give you? "My resignation", he said.

There are many people facing the new day who would like to resign for a while, even for a few hours. If only people would tell us how much they miss us now. But they forget. However, his eye is on the sparrow and I know he is watching me.

25 OCTOBER

Crispin and Crispinian – Italy – 4th century

Crispin and Crispinian were shoemakers. They had to earn their money with night work. During the day they were busy spreading the Good News of Jesus Christ to people in France. They were martyred. Some people say that our education system is good on ambition, but weak in ideals – that there is an overstress on excellence, with a loss to courtesy and sensitivity to the other person. The great writer and survivor of the Gulag, "Solzhenitsyn," says that when we forget God we lose balance.

26 OCTOBER

Cedd – England – 7th century

The most devilish temptation in the world is not the abuse of sex, drink or drugs. It is the wrong image we have of God as tyrant, judge, spy, spoilsport. The second worst temptation is the bad image we have of ourselves: "no good", "not nice", "victim". Jesus confronts both temptations head-on. "I bring Good News to the poor." The Father's compassionate love for all humanity. "I bring light to the blindness of low esteem, worthless feeling." You are a special creation – an original. There is none other like you. We're flawed, never perfect, but wonder-full – like children's coloured art work. Cedd was a monk living in solitude, but his vision of God's love for people pushed him out of the monastery to evangelise the poor. He was made Bishop by Finan at Lindisfarne. He founded monasteries at Bradwell, Tilbury and Lastingham. He built several churches.

27 OCTOBER

Frumentius – Syria – 4th century

There is a providence that guides our ways. Paul plants, Apollo waters, God gives the increase. But waiting is not always easy. Frumentius and his brother were on their way to India when their ship was attacked by natives in an African harbour. The local Ethopian king spared the lives of the two boys. Frumentius, when he grew to manhood, was appointed Treasurer of the Kingdom. When the King died Frumentius was given care of the education of the Royal Family. This gave him an opportunity to invite a Christian bishop. He made his request to St Athanasius, who appointed Frumentius himself as the bishop. Through his influence the young king was baptised. Many churches were built for the Ethiopian people.

28 OCTOBER

Jude – Palestine – 1st century

Why should we have to pray when God already knows what we need? St Augustine said we pray for our own good, to increase our desire, to be ready to receive God's gifts and blessings. He also said that prayer is more about groaning, than about words. Jude was chosen as a companion of Jesus, but he seems to hide from the light. We see little, or know little of him. His appeal is to the inner heart of people, people with deep desires, but shy with the weight of worry and inadequacy. He is patron of all of us who know little about prayer methods, but groan in the heart with a sense of helplessness, yet trusting in the compassionate Father who understands us.

29 OCTOBER

Bartholomew de las Casas – Spain – 16th century

Pope John Paul II wisely said, "Remember to respect people at their different stages of development in the journey of life." Yesterday a young man brought his two nieces in their teens to be christened. He said that he had re-found his faith. The Church is a sign. Sometimes people see little or nothing in the sign. Other times they see wonder and the finger of God. Bartholomew de las Casas did not see any injustice in being a slave-owner. It was only when he became a Dominican priest that he reluctantly had a complete change of mind and heart. He became the great champion of liberation.

30 OCTOBER

Alphonsus Rodriguez – Spain – 17th century

What a difference it makes – the way one answers the phone. In the business world people are schooled to be polite, pleasant and helpful on the phone. The most important person on a hospital staff, I have often thought, is the telephonist. The telephonist tries to ease the worries and fears of people for their sick ones, keeping lifelines open. Alphonsus Rodriguez regarded himself somewhat as a failure. He lost his wife and children. He joined the Jesuits as a doorkeeper. Every time a caller came or the doorbell rang, he said: "That's Christ calling, I'm coming, Lord."

31 OCTOBER

Gerard Majella – Italy – 18th century

I wonder how Gerard Majella became patron saint of childbirth. He was never married, nor did he have children. His gifts were tailoring and being a friend to the sick. He had a special way with the sinner and suffered false accusation himself. It is said that the person with a generous heart can take on any job in life. We long to be affirmed, thought sincerely of, listened to for ourselves. People who make us feel good are the real life-givers.

November

1 NOVEMBER

All Saints

A little child was fascinated by the wonderful colours in the church windows. He asked his dad about the people in the windows. "They are the saints", his dad explained. "But what are the saints", the little child asked persistently. Then suddenly he said, "I know, they are people that let the light shine through them." Ideas, imagination, memory are lights of mystery in every human person. Buried lights. We are privileged to enlighten one another through life. Smiles and compliments, instruction, guidance. All our lights are rekindled in some secret place.

2 NOVEMBER

All Souls

All Souls remind me that we only see death from one side – trial, pain, loss, tears. There is another side which tells that death is a friend that takes us through a door into the banquet of heaven, where tears are wiped away, darkness is no more and all is renewed. Our dear departed are near, but invisible.

3 NOVEMBER

Martin de Porres – Peru – 17th century

All the odds were against Martin. He was illegitimate and rejected by his father. He took on the most menial tasks to survive. He was barber, gardener, carer of the poor, collector of money, lover of animals and a lay Dominican Brother. Pope John XXIII said that Martin did all he could to care for the poor, farmhands, blacks and mulattos who were looked down on as slaves. Martin had God's vision of a world in harmony, but for harmony there is need of true justice in the way we relate to God, to self and to the world. It is said that Martin was the first saint to set up a home for pet animals – although it was in his sister's house. For him all is interrelated in God's plan – the cosmos, the animal kingdom, all humankind. We are, in a real sense, guests of this world.

4 NOVEMBER

Charles Borromeo – Italy – 16th century

Milan cherishes the memory of Borromeo. He lived and died for its people. His influence spread far beyond his native Italy. He brought the three "D's" to a church that was deflated and discouraged. The "D" of dedication, God's love. The "D" of discipline, love expressed in practical doing for each other. But he said do not spend yourself so completely on other people that you have nothing left for good of self. The third "D" was doctrine. There has to be a basic foundation and roots or else the fabric wobbles and there is confusion and panic. One of the great signs in today's world is the hunger for the face of the compassionate Father. The desire to respect the humanity of each other and the wish to translate God's love into a language that is hopeful and helpful for the day's march.

5 NOVEMBER

Zachary and Elizabeth – Palestine – 1st century

God's plan is always to bring life out of death, to bring life through darkness. The lives of Zachary and Elizabeth are outstanding proof that against all the odds, there is life and surprise. The compassionate Father delights in his sons and daughters. Elizabeth's womb is dead, yet the great John the Baptist is born. Zachary is struck dumb in disbelief, yet he can sing the greatest love song ever penned, in the name of John the Baptist:

"Blest be the Lord, he has visited his people and redeemed them, he has raised up for us a mighty Saviour. This is the loving kindness of the heart of our God."

Through the dark and painful days of life, when we are disheartened by happenings and overcome with weakness, Zachary and Elizabeth give us lifelines of trust in the loving kindness of the heart of our God.

6 NOVEMBER

All the Saints of Ireland

An Irish American searching for his family roots visited a ruined cemetery. An old man explained: "If the year is 1840, you haven't a chance of finding a trace or a name. People were too poor to mark their dead with a monument or headstone. They were given to the earth with the sign of the cross." I think of those unnamed people as the saints of Ireland. They lived lives unnoticed, without claim and yet passed on to us great traditions of respect, hospitality and joviality. They too were privileged to be born, to be chosen to enlighten this world with their presence, their ideas, their imagination. We, like them, are encouraged in believing that nothing is lost, that there is this sacred place where all one's experiences are gathered in the light of God's mercy.

7 NOVEMBER

Willibrord – England – 8th century

The branches, the flowers, the corn, bend with the wind. It is the price of survival. Rigidity breaks under pressure. The tension of life can break us if we take it all too seriously. Willibrord had strength in flexibility. Leaving a monastery in Ripon, he spent twelve years in Ireland in the company of Egbert. He took on mission work in Holland and Denmark with eleven other monks. He related to the Pope and the civil rulers of the day. He saw his missionary work destroyed by the usurper Radbod.

When Radbod died he went back into Friesland, and began his work all over again.

8 NOVEMBER

Godfrey – France – 11th century

God is full of surprises and draws people to himself in all kinds of different ways. Sometimes we narrow God's imagination, thinking that God is found only in certain areas like Mass, the sacraments, Mary, but God's mercy is much wider than we imagine. Sometimes we can underrate the spirituality of so many people whose devotion is not fed on the observances we have been used to. Godfrey was an outstanding monk and a reformer of monasteries. But when he became a bishop, the same methods did not work well for him. He was seen as harsh and inhuman. One person's honey can be another person's poison. We rely on the spirit of Jesus to help us with right prescriptions when celebrating human nature in all its wonder and complexity.

9 NOVEMBER

Caravaggio – Italy – 16th century

The great artist Caravaggio has a fascination for hands. Perhaps he saw his own humanity in terms of hands – the creative open hand that brings light to the world. The closed fist that brings pain and destruction. There is always the mix of the seed and the weed that is our redeemed humanity. In his masterpiece "The Taking of Christ" vicious hands encircle the victim, while the hands of Christ are at peace. Caravaggio reflects attentively on the Gospel story which says: "They handed him over." Jesus Christ now seems to be inactive, passive, waiting on the hands of others – in the hands of others. So much of our lives are like that; we depend on the hands of others, not only in childhood, but through the years of life. Often there is little we can do about our own personality, our limitations, our illness, our old age, our family, friends or neighbours. We can only wait. Is Jesus saying that silent, trusting waiting is Godlike, in a world where activity is glorified? "They also serve who only stand and wait."

10 NOVEMBER

Leo the Great – Italy – 5th century

Leo the Great defended the Church on two fronts. There was the inner battle for truth and there was the outer battle of invading armies at the gates of Rome. He placated the enemy, but was a defender of truth. He was a man who knew the world as flawed and corrupt, yet it was the place where the Kingdom of God was present and active. In baptism we enjoy a dignity common to us all, he said. His respect for the human person was deep. It is said that the true Church is the one that is seen to care most for the human person. Jesus asked: "Who do you think was the neighbour to the one who fell among the robbers?"

11 NOVEMBER

Martin of Tours – Hungary – 4th century

Martin must be one of the great characters of the Heavenly Kingdom. He gave up army life saying, "I am a soldier of Christ, it is not lawful for me to fight." He lived as a monk and set up one of the first monasteries at Poitiers. The people demanded that he be their bishop and tricked him into taking that responsibility. Some people thought that his scruffy hair and shaggy appearance wasn't a good sign. He was a compassionate man, who pleaded with the Emperor for Priscillian and his followers, who were accused of being a threat to the State with their radical ideas. While still a soldier, he gave half his precious cloak to a beggar and saw Christ wearing the half cloak, in Heaven, in a dream. His prayer was, "Lord if your people still need me, praised be your good will."

12 NOVEMBER

Josaphat Byelorussia – Poland – 16th century

Josaphat wanted to be a bridge-builder between east and west, bringing Orthodox Slavs back to communion with Rome. In his work to restore unity, he was set upon and murdered. Bridge-building with nations, peacemaking with people, always involves struggles and tensions. Parents are the great peacemakers in ordinary life, because there is need for deep understanding of the person. The strengths and weaknesses, also sensitivity to fears. Unity allows for diversity. Uniformity is fixed and restricted.

13 NOVEMBER

Frances Xavier Cabrini – Italy – 20th century

When I was invited to celebrate the anniversary Mass for priests who were fifty, forty and ten years ordained, the immediate instinct was to refuse, and the reason – fear of being a failure or thought foolish. I was helped to face the fear with a thought that it was a good opportunity to say thanks. Frances Cabrini became the first citizen of the United States to be canonised. She followed Italian immigrants to the US, to help them through schools, hospitals and orphanages. When she ran into housing problems, the Archbishop of New York advised her to return home. She didn't. She faced the fear and the problem. She dreaded water. Yet she crossed the Atlantic thirty times because the love in her heart was greater than the fear of the water. She thanked God with her practicality.

14 NOVEMBER

Laurence O'Toole – Dublin – 12th century

Laurence was a man for all seasons, a hostage, an Abbot of Glendalough, Archbishop, peace negotiator with Henry II and survivor of a murderous assault in Canterbury. Despite his best efforts, he failed to keep troubles out of Ireland. With Kevin of Glendalough he is the patron of Dublin diocese. It is said that he prayed in Kevin's cell overlooking the two lakes of Glendalough in times of trouble. The Good Lord tells us that obstacles will often come our way in the journey of life. But we must not make obstacles for others. When asked we are to forgive often. Jesus said: be like the mustard seed, small, dependant, but trusting in God's merciful providence. Laurence caught that spirit.

15 NOVEMBER

Albert the Great – Germany – 13th century

Albert was a prodigy, a walking encyclopaedia and a man of immense knowledge. For him science and the love of God were not opposites, but two sides of the one coin of truth. Religion needs science to keep the mind alert. Science needs religion to focus on wonder and respect and the God of surprises. Our world is full of different presences. God encircles the world with his love. Mass was a focal point and highlight in the life of Albert. He said that nothing could be more healthy than celebrating the Mass to the memory of Jesus who said: "Do this." His love of God prompted him to challenge illiteracy and poverty in every shape and form.

16 NOVEMBER

Gertrude the Great – Spain – 13th century

Gertrude found the Sacred Heart of Jesus in her study of the Sacred Scriptures – God's word. The love of Christ in his humanity overwhelmed her. She spoke of the prodigal daughter alongside the prodigal son. God's mercy and love includes all. The spirit of Gertrude has rekindled and opened for us new treasures of God's word, through the teaching of the Second Vatican Council. God's word in human language is an endless source of strength, encouragement, hope and wisdom.

17 NOVEMBER

Elizabeth of Hungary – 13th century

To marry at 14 years of age, have three children in a very loving relationship with her husband Louis, to be widowed in her twenties and to die at 24 is a very interesting story. Her love of the poor took over her life. She kept just one old dress for her burial. We can underestimate the capacity of young people for goodness. A man who climbed Everest said: "If you think you can do it, you can do it." The heart that's in love works miracles. Elizabeth was deeply in love with God, and saw God's love in everything. She passed on God's love to his loved ones.

18 NOVEMBER

Peter and Paul Basilicas

What attracts in people is often vulnerability and charm. To be human is a mix of light and shade. Peter is big-hearted, ready to take risks. He jumps into the water for his friend. He is flawed, but we never doubt his good intention. He fights, runs away, cries. Yet he has the loyalty of genuine love. Paul is an intellectual genius, with the stamina of a lion. Proud of his Jewish blood, he is enthusiastic in persecuting the new religion that he sees as threat. But after his conversion experience on the road to Damascus, he is equally enthusiastic and overwhelmed with the love of Christ that is to be found in the everyday person. This message of love was burned into his heart with the words: "Saul, why do you persecute me?"

19 NOVEMBER

Margaret of Scotland – 11th century

The artist Van Gogh painted a picture of shoes with loosened laces. Although each shoe is separate and different, they are united together somehow, in an awesome beauty. There is loveliness in their texture, despite the signs of wear and tear, and the struggles of life. The laces that tie to the duty of life are now loosened, and somehow reflect peace and the serenity of "mission accomplished". Margaret of Scotland and Malcolm, her husband, were always like two left shoes in their contrasting gifts, but they made a unit of their relationship. Blessed with eight children, she was deeply charitable and a lover of the poor. He helped her ambition. His roughness was refined through the miracle of love. Paul says: "Love is patient, kind, believes all things, hopes all things, endures all things. Love never ends."

20 NOVEMBER

Jimmy Dolan – Ferbane, Ireland – 20th century

Jimmy Dolan looms large on my private calendar of saints. He encouraged me to play football when I was a youngster. He would borrow a pair of football boots and a jersey for me, which only the exceptional family would own in those days. He was the local postman. He always encouraged us to play a clean game. He rubbed his hands vigorously when he was excited. I never heard a foul or condemnatory word from his lips. He fought to get his charges on the minor county team. This distinction was paradise on earth for a young person. Through football I met many friends. But perhaps even more blessed, the football gave me a healthy self-confidence, which proved a great support during dark and cloudy days of failing exams and feelings of inadequacy. There are many walking saints who surround our lives; some are called parents, grandparents, teachers, nurses. There is no end to the list. I thank God for this great person who was a lifeline of blessing for me.

21 NOVEMBER

Presentation of the Blessed Virgin Mary

People like to think of Mary's birth being celebrated on this day. We invited the school infants to come to see the baptismal font in our church where their birth was celebrated. We composed a poem together:

"When I was born my parents were glad.
They brought me to church to say thanks to God.
They blessed me with water in the name of the Three –
Father, Son and Holy Spirit are special friends to me."

Mary prays for us to respect life and celebrate people who are God's delight.

22 NOVEMBER

Cecilia – Rome – 2nd century

Cecilia is thought of as a happy person and patron of music. It is not easy to understand happiness in the midst of martyrdom. A piece of sculpture I saw represented a martyred person, lying peacefully and beautifully, but with three fingers raised in praise of God, who is Father, Son and Spirit. It is as if one hand is always held in God's hand. Baptism for Cecilia was a real presence of God who is Father, Son and Spirit. "The sacred three my fortress be, come encircle me."

23 NOVEMBER

Columban – Ireland – 6th century

I experienced Columban's hospitality before I ever knew the story of Columban. As a young seminarian, who was neither fish nor flesh, I never forget the invitations of the Columban Community to play football games and join their festivity. Years later, as a priest doing immigrant work in London, I experienced the same hospitality and welcome from the Columban priests, who offered practical help to immigrants, meeting new arrivals, organising accommodation and work. Their house was a home away from home. They never lost the spirit of their founder. It is said that Columban was a warm hearted man. The greatness of his love pushed him far beyond the shores of Ireland. He took on kings and kingdoms for the love of his God. His last stop was Bobbio in northern Italy. In his last days he took an active part in building his church.

24 NOVEMBER

Colman – Ireland – 6th century

I have a good friend who was a student of St Colman's College in Co. Cork. Like Colman, he is a poet and a bard. He loves to sing a song and excels in recitation. He is full of hospitality. It is said that Brendan of Kerry baptised Colman of Cork when Colman was 50 years of age. It is good to remember that youthfulness is in the mind and spirit, rather than in years. Brendan and Colman were forever youthful because of their ideals. Finding one's true self is not being selfish, it is rather to discover that all is given in life and that we have the extraordinary privilege of using our gifts and talents to make a better world; to say the word of praise, to do the good turn, to be happy for others.

25 NOVEMBER

Pope John 23rd – Italy – 20th century

Pope John gives me great encouragement. In the twilight of his life he renewed and refreshed the whole world – pointed us in the direction of God, the compassionate Father. During the Second Vatican Council, John was anxious, and could not sleep one night. A voice said to him: "Is it you or me that's running the Church, John?" "All right", John answered, and fell fast asleep. In his dying hours, his secretary called to see him. John said to his secretary: "When all this fuss is over, make sure you go home to see your mother." It is good to remember that there is one Saviour and it is not you or me. He teaches us to be carefree, because we trust in the good God.

26 NOVEMBER

Catherine of Alexandria – Egypt

Sister Wendy Beckett reflects on Lorenzo Lotto's masterpiece of Catherine of Alexandria. The spiked wheel that was the instrument of her torture is scarcely visible. She is serene, almost smiling at us, and beautifully arrayed like a princess. The ring on her finger hints at the secret of her peace. God is her lover. Knowing God's love, she is able to trust, despite torture and trials. The same God surrounds our life and our daily happenings. Lord, you are our refuge and our strength.

27 NOVEMBER

Virgilius – Ireland – 8th century

Imagination is surely an awesome gift. We are given access to so many worlds. The early Irish monks were wanderers for God. They were imaginative people. Virgilius wandered to Salzburg in Austria, and built a fine cathedral there. The wonder of God enlightened him to think that there were other mysterious worlds – that there were different presences of God beyond our dreams and imagination. Indeed when one looks long enough at a sunrise or dawn over the sea, with clouds of ever changing colours and shapes, one is prompted to ask "Why not?" Virgilius' ideas got him into a bit of trouble, but I guess, it was worth the risk. Better to have tried and lost, than never to have tried at all.

28 NOVEMBER

Catherine Labouré – France – 19th century

Catherine never went to school because her mother died when she was 8 years old. Catherine liked minding chickens and opening doors for hospitality. When she entered religious life, in the service of the poor, she had a vision of the Blessed Mother, with two hands outstretched, giving blessings to the world to all who ask. A medal with two Ms was made to celebrate her experience. I noticed the bride at a recent wedding wearing this medal of Mary. The Sisters of St Vincent de Paul carry on the loving and caring spirit of Catherine, whose family name was Zoe.

29 NOVEMBER

Thomas Merton – USA – 20th century

Thomas Merton is called the great American of our times. He is for many the outstanding small saint of this century – God's bridge-builder in his ideas, humanity, compassion. Although a Trappist monk he loved God's world and all God's people. On a visit to Louisville one day he watched hundreds of people milling about. He was suddenly overwhelmed with the realisation that he loved all these people. He wrote something like this: "I suddenly saw the secret beauty of their hearts, the core reality, the person each one is in God's eyes. If only they could see each other as they are, there would be no more war, hatred, greed, but that cannot be seen, only believed. At our death is a point, a spark, which belongs entirely to God. The point is his name written in us. It is in everybody. The gate of heaven is everywhere." What really matters he said, "is openness to face risk." You don't need to know precisely what is going on, or exactly where it is going. What you need is to recognise the possibilities and challenges offered at the moment. Courage here is love.

30 NOVEMBER

Andrew – Palestine – 1st century

The artist Duccio painted a masterpiece of the Lord calling Andrew and Peter. Both are in the boat of life. Both are engaged in hauling their nets, but they are different individuals, responding in different ways. Peter seems ready for action, willing to risk, to have a go. Andrew seems more thoughtful, mystical and contemplative. All human beings are both active and contemplative. The best flowering of a tree is when the inner roots are in tune with the outer branches and leaves. Without inner strength there is imbalance. There is an inner me that worries, fears, frets, like a prisoner in a cell. There is also an inner me that smiles, compliments and appreciates the day. The wonder is that God inhabits both me's. God loves the mix and mess of humanity. Andrew listens to the Lord before he introduces Peter to him. Andrew also spots the little boy with the small gift that feeds the multitudes.

December

1 DECEMBER

Edmund Campion – England – 16th century

Edmund Campion was chosen to give the welcoming speech to Queen Elizabeth when she visited Oxford. He went to Dublin to help found Trinity College and also to resolve his doubts about his Protestant religion. At the English college in Douai, France, he became Catholic. He joined the Jesuit Order in Rome. He was ordained priest in Prague where he lectured. He was sent to set up a Jesuit mission in England, to help dispirited Catholics. He disguised himself as a jewel merchant. He ministered to the poor and prisoners throughout England, as a hunted priest. He was betrayed. A prejudiced jury and discredited witnesses condemned him to death. In his last speech he said: "In condemning us, you condemn all your own ancestors." His loyalty to the Queen was clear. He offence was his religious conscience.

2 DECEMBER

Ruth, Old Testament

Ruth is a fond favourite, a Christmas Saint. Naomi lost her husband and two sons in Moab. She longed to go back to her own people in Bethlehem, to die. Ruth, her daughter-in-law, pledged to go with her, to leave her own people for a foreign land, and also forfeit an opportunity for marriage. The words of Ruth become to Naomi a wedding song: "Wherever you go I shall go. Wherever you live so shall I live. Your people will be my people and your God will be my God too." Ruth would not take no for an answer. But God is never outdone in generosity or surprises. In Bethlehem Boaz, a wealthy farmer, spots his dream girl – Ruth. There is a marriage. Ruth becomes the great grandmother of David – and Jesus is of the family of David. Death or setback is only a comma, not a full stop in God's providence.

3 DECEMBER

Francis Xavier – Spain – 16th century

Francis fell under the spell of Ignatius Loyola when he was in Paris. He became a priest and a missionary, bringing the Good News of Christ to Asia, Japan and India. His boat journey to India took thirteen months. He was a human, practical and humorous man. His workload was sensational. He would ring a small bell to attract children and people to hear his message. "I let them in by their own door," he said, "but I see to it that they come out by mine." The original communities that he set up survived after his time, in spite of waves of attack and persecution. He saw himself as sowing the seed, an instrument in God's hand. Only God gives the increase. We are called to be instruments of God's goodness, to do what we can, where we are, with what we have.

4 DECEMBER

Rembrandt – Holland – 17th century

Rembrandt is one of my favourite chosen people. His master painting "The Return of the Prodigal Son" is a world treasure. Only a man who has suffered deeply in his own heart could gift us with such a jewel. He paints the compassionate, healing God our Father, who hugs in his warm cloak the returned son who kneels like a convict, faceless, footless and in tatters. The Prodigal Son had made up his confession, but he never got a chance to use it. The Father's hands – one male, one female – embrace him generously, not possessively. God's love is all. The older son stands resentful and not able to share the joyful reunion. The father loves him too – "All I have is yours!" The message is stunning – God does not reject anyone, in fact it would be impossible for God to reject any of his loved ones.

5 DECEMBER

Karl Rahner – Germany – 20th century

Years of dust and grit had dulled Rembrandt's masterpiece. When it was restored to its original beauty and colour, some people were disappointed. They had grown so used to the discoloured masterpiece, that their eyes had become dulled to loveliness. I think of Karl Rahner as a restorer of discoloured ideas and images about God the Father. He said that God's grace is for all people, at all times, and is not restricted to Christians.

Maybe, he said, we have looked at other peoples and other religions and cultures with too little love. The experience of God lies hidden within every human experience. Our lives are intertwined in absolute mystery. We experience God by experiencing ourselves and other people. We are graced sinners. The implicit liturgy of our daily lives becomes explicit when we celebrate at church. The Catholic Church wrote many of his ideas into the documents of the Second Vatican Council.

6 DECEMBER

Hosea, Old Testament

Hosea is really a Christmas saint and a fond favourite among many. Married to Gomer, he had three children. Gomer was restless and became a prostitute. Hosea still loved her, and in the strength of his love for her, wooed her back to be his wife again. Through this experience Hosea began to realise how God feels about us and our unfaithfulness. Through him God says to us, "How can I abandon you? You are my heart's desire. My love for you is too strong." The message of Jesus is not just words, quotations or stories from 2,000 years ago, it is an ever-present love, fresh, new, surprising and for us.

7 DECEMBER

Ambrose – Germany – 4th century

Could you imagine a man being appointed bishop, even though he was not baptised and had not made his First

Communion? Ambrose was the popular choice of the laity of Milan to be their bishop because of his ability as a peacemaker. There is certainly endless variety within the Church of God. We can only admire God's bad taste and funny choices. Ambrose was really one of the great human beings of this world in mind and heart. He was poet, orator and tough negotiator. Not least, he influenced the wayward Augustine, whose change of heart still ripples our lives in many ways. Let your words be full of understanding, Ambrose said. A good thought for the day.

8 DECEMBER

The Immaculate Conception of Mary

John MacQuarrie, the Anglican scholar, writes inspirationally about Mary, our Blessed Mother. Mary is an entirely human person, he says. The great artist Velazquez tells more about the Immaculate Conception than many of our writings and ideas. Mary is suffused in light and colour – idealised – but totally human. MacQuarrie prefers to think of Mary as always being preserved in a right relationship with God, rather than being preserved from a stain. When Jesus walked this earth he spoke of justice as right relationships with God, with self, with others and the world. This was the meaning of the Father's Kingdom. Mary was God's most faithful and just disciple all through her life.

9 DECEMBER

Juan Diego – Mexico – 16th century

The bishop was not impressed with Juan Diego's story of seeing the Virgin Mary. Juan was prompted to go to the mountain, in wintertime, and pick up roses, for the bishop. When Juan opened his cloak to present the flowers, an image of Mary had been traced on the cloak. I like Our Lady's imagination of giving roses to a bishop. Roses do work miracles of love and friendship. The Lady said to Juan: "Don't be afraid of any pain, illness or accident." I like Mary's positive message, that God is with us through the trials and struggles of life. Juan Diego tells us that Mary always prays for us, now and at the hour of our death.

10 DECEMBER

Catherine McAuley – Ireland – 19th century

Catherine McAuley found her God in people's faces – wherever there was a human need. Her religious rule of life was simply loving people in God's love. She wanted to be a "walkabout" nun, rather than an enclosed religious. With others, she longed to help people in practical ways. She knew poverty and riches, but it was people that mattered most. Whether it was her Quaker friends, Daniel O'Connell, the Liberator, or the deprived girls and children of Baggot Street.

Her name is fondly remembered in the oldest streets and places of Dublin – Grand Canal Road, Townsend Street,

Clarendon Street, Cooper Alley, Merchant's Quay, St Paul's, Arran Quay, the ProCathedral, Mary Street, Henry Street, Liffey Street, George's Hill, Jervis Street.

Her Sisters have brought her caring spirit to all five continents through teaching and concern for the sick and underprivileged. Her kindly eyes look at us through the face of today's Irish Five Pound Note. She said that the demands of the poor and the keeping of appointments were the greatest penance. She recommended a piano for entertainment among her Sisters. When she was dying she reminded the Sisters to make sure to have a nice cup of tea when all was over and God would comfort them.

11 DECEMBER

Damasus – Spain – 4th century

Not least of Damasus' distinctions was that he wrote his own funeral speech: "He who calms the waves and gives life to dying seeds in the earth, and loosed Lazarus from the darkness of his chains, will make Damasus rise again from the dust." Jesus stressed living life before death, as the best recipe for the Kingdom. Damasus certainly lived for the day and praised its blessings. A pagan by birth, his choice as Pope was violently contested. He lived under the shadow of an anti-Pope and his supporters. He encouraged St Jerome to make the Scriptures available to all of us. He restored the catacombs to the memory of Christian martyrs and shortened the Mass.

12 DECEMBER

Jane Frances de Chantel – France – 17th century

There is only one vocation. That is to love. Jane Frances knew a lot about love. She was happily married, with children. Her husband died tragically. She was very depressed under the tyranny of her father-in-law. She met St Francis de Sales. Their friendship gave new purpose to her life. She set up a religious community of women who would visit the sick and the poor, and pray together. She spoke about the white martyrdom of living life with love. So many people we see every day are martyrs for love. They allow themselves to be disturbed for others, coping with children and teen families. One saint said that parents with children are excused from prayer because their life is a prayer, a kind of martyrdom of love.

13 DECEMBER

Lucy – Italy – 4th century

Perugino has painted a beautiful picture of St Lucy. He concentrated on Lucy's eyes, looking steadfastly heavenwards towards God. She is single-minded and single-hearted in her love, and wants to remain single for God's sake. She is martyred. She holds in her right hand the book of God's Word and in her left a chalice of flame – the expression of love. Mass celebrates the Word of God, the Book, and the sacrifice of Jesus, the Chalice. The Word of God enlightens the mind about God's never-failing love for his wayward sons and daughters. True love always wants to express itself in giving for others – the everyday caring of life with family, friends, neighbours and far-away friends. The Eucharist celebrates God and people.

14 DECEMBER

John of the Cross – Spain – 16th century

Toledo, Avila, Segovia recall the memory of John of the Cross. His own religious people had him imprisoned in Toledo with nine months of harsh treatment, almost in total darkness. He escaped. During this darkness he wrote with the heart of a mystic, poetic and spiritual ideas that are a treasure to our world. He became the friend of St Teresa of Avila. Their friendship encouraged each other. Opting out is a popular word in today's world. When the going gets tough, when difficulties arise, there is always the temptation to run away, to blame the world, rather than dig deep into one's inner resources. Teresa of Avila advised John not to opt out for a more religious way of life, by joining the Carthusians. Stay within your own family, renew and transform it. John's and Teresa's new ideas were not acceptable to many people, but they were full of truth and life-giving. Jesus said that the prophet is not acceptable in his own family, or by his own people. So to be on the losing side is not always a failure.

15 DECEMBER

Venantius – Italy – 6th century

Venantius loved singing songs and writing poems. When he was chaplain to the nuns in Potieries he wrote letters and poems to Abbess Agnes and Sister Radequend. To Radequend, who was quite elderly, he wrote: "Even though clouds are gone and the sky is serene, the day is sunless without you. When I can, I will send roses and lilies." He was elected Bishop of Potieries. Sometimes it takes courage to compliment people. I think the charm of Jesus was that he always saw good in people no matter how odd, different or unacceptable they thought they were. It is said that Venantius had his eyes healed when he was younger. We need a healing for insight, the insight that helps us to praise. God's first words to Mary were a compliment, followed by the assurance, "Don't be afraid."

16 DECEMBER

Isaiah – born 765 BC

The days before Christmas evoke the memory of God's prophets. The prophet was God's friend, chosen to interpret God's word now; to tell how to live in the present world. Because the truth is sometimes bitter and hard to take, the prophets were often misunderstood and rejected. Despite all the harsh realities and disasters of the times, the prophets always held high the candle of hope, of God's mercy, love and forgiveness. Isaiah gave dire warnings because God's people had become over-rich and were exploiting the helpless and the poor. God says – not fair. That's the bad news. The good news is that God never forgets his sinful people: "You will return from your prison and exile, so rejoice, take off your dress of sorrow, put on the beauty of the glory of God, put a crown of glory on your head. Now God brings you back, back like royal princes. There is joy in the light of God's mercy."

17 DECEMBER

Jeremiah – born 646 BC

Jeremiah challenged the system. It was corrupt, he said. The people will destroy themselves by their behaviour. He was tagged "traitor". He was thrown into a well to die. He cursed the day that he was born and said that he never wanted to do this job for God, but God's message was like a restless fire in his heart. "I say I will forget the Lord, then your message is like a fire burning in me, I can't keep it back." Yet as the world collapses all around him Jeremiah sings of hope. "A branch will grow from the dark tree of our humanity. Its flower will be the Saviour of all peoples. All humankind will see the salvation of God."

18 DECEMBER

Micah – 8th century BC

Bad religion is worse than no religion. God's people got contaminated with bad religion. Blinded by superstitious religious practices, they failed to be just, kind and merciful. They forgot the God of justice and compassion. God did not want their animal sacrifices or their mechanical empty worship, Micah said: "Act justly, love tenderly, walk humbly before the Lord." As always, the prophet tells of God's hope and love for his people, despite all their misgivings. Down the centuries he says, there will be Bethlehem, an insignificant town of yours that will give a Saviour for the world. Lift up your hearts. The challenge to change direction is a comma in God's language. The assurance of hope and constant mercy is the full stop.

19 DECEMBER

Jonah – 5th century BC

I like the Jonah story. It is God's way of telling us about his compassionate mercy. Jonah did not want to be a prophet. He tried his best to get out of the job, but God is a persistent lover, and does not seem to mind our ridiculous antics. Somehow our inner core is love-tagged to his heart with the words "My Delightful One". Jonah refuses to talk of God's love to the Ninevites, because in his mind they are undesirables. He skips to sea, but God hooks him in the whale. Then he goes reluctantly to the city of Nineveh, but he tries to paint a bad picture of God. To his surprise the people change their ways and become a loving community. God's mercy is much broader than our small minds.

20 DECEMBER

Zephaniah – born 640 BC

God's people had sunk deeper into violence and empty religious practices. Zephaniah saw the writing on the wall and cried out: "There will be trouble and distress and destruction. A black and cloudy day is upon us." That's the challenge, and then comes a guarantee of God's forever loving kindness despite the crooked ways of humanity. Zephaniah calls out: "Shout for joy, people of Zion, the Lord has repealed your sentence. The Lord is in your midst. My people, have no fear, do not let your hands fall limp, your God is in your midst. He will exult with joy over you. He will renew you by his love. He will dance with shouts of joy for you." What a God!

21 DECEMBER

Anastasia – Italy – 4th century

The name Anastasia rings a happy bell for me. I was scared taking on a new appointment in the vast city of London, in St Aloysius Parish. Anastasia was a nun in the nearby convent. She opened doors all day long and worked preparing meals in the kitchen from morning to night. She always wore a smile of welcome and enthused about one's well being, taking out little niceties of food to make one feel good. She suffered a lot with headaches and never talked about her own pain, but should you mention your cold or headache, she always had something soothing to offer. We don't know much about her namesake martyr Anastasia. It is said that she was put out to sea in a boat and abandoned, and Atheodota, of dubious character, rescued her. My Anastasia also put out to sea as a young girl. She found peace and prayer doing ordinary, simple things with love. She had a good friend whose name was Martina. The hidden goodness and prayer of such lives, of absence from so much, fills the world with blessings, unknown and unheard of, and, it is said, holds back waves of evil that mysteriously threaten us.

22 DECEMBER

Mozart – 18th century

Mozart was a gifted genius in the world of music. His ability to lift the heart, refresh the spirit, to distil joy, is beyond compare. His musical career began at four years of age. He suffered disappointments and rejections during his short life. He was buried in a common grave. Yet his light-hearted spirit continues to grace our world with magical sound. He died in his 30's and he wrote this letter to his father in 1778.

"Dear Father, since death is the ultimate purpose of life, I have made myself acquainted with this real friend of mankind. I am not frightened, rather comforted and consoled. I never lie down to sleep without thinking, young as I am, that I may not live to see another day. I will not be saddened or unwilling when the time comes. For this happiness I thank my Creator every day. I wish the same happiness to everyone in my life."

The words are as beautiful as his farewell requiem.

23 DECEMBER

Amos – born 760 BC

Times were good under King Jeroboam. Peace and plenty, strong currency, good trade and extensive building. There was no religious persecution. Amos, lowly shepherd, was called by God to spotlight the oncoming disaster. Wealth was with the few, deadening poverty suffocated many. The rich were outwardly very religious, but there was a serious rot inside. Amos does not hold back: "The rich sell the virtuous person for silver, the poor man for a pair of sandals. You trample on the poor, extracting unjust levies. Your houses of dressed stone will never be lived in, nor will you drink the wine of your precious vineyards. I hate your feasts, I take no pleasure in your solemn festivals. So no more of your din of chanting or strumming on harps, let justice and honesty flow like water." Yet his words are like those of a caring parent chiding the child, wanting to draw out the best and to reassure with love. God says, "I mean to restore the fortunes of my people, I will rebuild their ruined cities and they will live in them, never to be uprooted again from the land I will give them."

24 DECEMBER

Mary – Awaiting the Christ Child

Josep Heinzmann writes, imagining Mary pondering in her heart:

"My own people have told me, O God, that you are so exalted above everything that exists, that I dare not even to pronounce your name, that I will die if I presume to approach your presence; and now you, yourself, have made your way into the narrow confines of my womb. In me you have sunk your roots as a human person. In me you have taken a new name Emmanuel – God with us – and you are my child. My people Israel have experienced your wonderful deeds. You were with my people. You guided them and set them free. Our fathers told me the wonderful stories of your love and now this history has taken on human flesh within me. I am privileged to bear, within myself, both the memory of your many great works and also the fulfilment of your unheard-of promises."

25 DECEMBER

Jesus of Nazareth

Jesus of Nazareth, the carpenter's son, is not a gloomy moraliser, nor a zealot, not a man out of touch with reality. He enjoys flowers in the meadow and birds in the sky. He observes the farmer when he sows and when he reaps. He is familiar with everyday activities and the customs of his people. His love is tender, practical and never theoretical. He has sympathy for the poor, the sick and the outcast; knows how to be happy, how to cry and how to tremble with anxiety and agony. Strangers and foreigners, too, he draws into his spell – we want to see Jesus, the men from Greece say. Even his enemies are impressed because he teaches God's way of life sincerely. Jesus is wholly other – he accepts the despised, the humble, the public sinners in friendship. He calls little children to him. He stands by the adulterous woman when everyone else is condemning her. He turns away from honour and glory when they try to make him king. He accepts a dinner invitation from a hated tax collector, an unmistakable sign of friendship. He allows a prostitute to anoint his feet while he is at dinner in the home of a respectable family. He speaks with a Samaritan woman, even though this is certain to be taken as heresy. He does not shrink from touching the lepers, even though they are outcasts from human society. He holds his peace when they mock and scourge him. His teaching and preaching turn everything upside down and shock his audience. Love your enemies, do good to those who hate you. He is a contradiction to the established order of his day. He has a weakness for the weak. He himself lives from the vantage point of a wholly unique relationship with God the Father.

26 DECEMBER

Stephen – Palestine – 1st century

An ideal Christian dream is to show the attractiveness of God to others and to believe oneself. It is fitting that

Stephen's Day follows immediately after the Birth of Christ Day. Stephen died for an attractive God, with words of forgiveness on his lips. "They know not what they do." We all carry hurts from the past, some of our own making, some thrust upon us. It is a fond wish to be able to forgive oneself for never being perfect, to forgive others for their imperfections, and to thank God for his bad (good) taste in loving us just the way we are.

27 DECEMBER

John the Evangelist – Palestine – 1st century

Velazquez's painting of John catches his character. His eyes and mind are riveted heavenward. John was the closest friend of Jesus. He sat beside him at the Last Supper celebration. John sees deepest into the heart of Christ, which is a reservoir of goodness. John does not say God loves, he says "God is love", knows nothing else, cannot be different. To accept God's love is Christian faith, but it is a love to be found on every human face, a love that finds expression in our caring for each other. John is blunt, he says: "To say one loves God and hate the neighbour is lying." Yet Velazquez's painting tells us that it is not something we can do alone. We need help, but God gives us the assurance of his help. John is pleading and waiting, pen in hand, ready for action, but conscious that he is so dependant on God saying the word. In old age John repeated the same sermon always – "Little children, love one another."

28 DECEMBER

Solomon's Song (Song of Songs) – 5th century BC

God's love song to us is very passionate indeed and reminds us that sexuality is God's idea first:

"Your love is more delightful than wine.
Delicate is the fragrance of your perfume.
How beautiful you are, my love, how beautiful
you are.
His left arm is under my head, his right arm
embraces me.
Come, my lovely one, come, the winter is past,
the rains are over, flowers appear on earth,
show me your face, let me hear your voice,
for your voice is sweet and your face is beautiful,
you ravish my heart with a single one of your glances.
Love is a flash of fire, a flame of Yahweh God himself."

In God's love song are all love songs and all desires of our human hearts.

29 DECEMBER

Thomas Becket – England – 12th century

Thomas Becket, the one-time friend of King Henry II, became a thorn in the king's side when Thomas resisted the usurpation of church rights by the king. Henry wished to be rid of this troublesome priest. Four knights took the king's wishes to heart and murdered Becket in his own cathedral. Thomas, from day one, was a very popular saint among the people. Perhaps it was his humanity, more than his martyrdom, that appealed to the people. It is said that he took a nap every day in order the better to apply his body and mind to the duties of life. It is sad that many people have to wait for serious illness and doctor's orders before they begin to befriend the body with a cat-nap.

30 DECEMBER

Nicholas – Asia Minor (Turkey) – 4th century

There are many exciting stories told about Nicholas' generosity: how he gave three bags of gold to three ladies for their dowries, to save them from hardship. He is also the Santa Claus saint. The great artist Veronese selects a different item from his life for his painting. He is being made a bishop. Nicholas resists this privilege, but he is the man selected by the people and the priests. So the artist showed Nicholas almost being dragged to the altar for his consecration. He cannot escape. Heaven approves of the choice, because the angels carry the bishop's vestments for the consecration. The consecrating bishop lords it over Nicholas with a hand of blessing. Nicholas pleads to heaven; his eyes resting on the processional cross of the crucified Saviour. God will direct his life. He submits, only because it is through Christ's death and resurrection that Nicholas will succeed and survive.

31 DECEMBER

Sylvester – Italy – 4th century

Sylvester was the thirty-third Pope. He lived at the same time as the Emperor Constantine, whose victory marked a new day for the Church, with the ending of persecution, and freedom to express the Christian faith. Basilicas were built and the Nicene Creed was written into the Eucharistic celebration. Our ultimate goal is the new day of paradise. No word or image can express the joyful surprise of heaven. The Good Lord used the language of wedding and banquet when all kinds and all sorts are together in harmony, with fullness of life and complete joy. The famous prayer of Sylvester tells us:

"Nor shall we be without the world, that was home and mother to us. For all will be transformed into a new heaven and new earth. Lord, guide us always in this present life, and bring us to the joy that never ends."